EX LIBRIS

VINTAGE **CLASSICS**

VINTAGE CLASSICS

THE GREAT FIRE OF LONDON

Adrian Tinniswood is the author of fourteen books of social and architectural history. A Senior Research Fellow at the University of Buckingham and a Visiting Fellow in Heritage and History at Bath Spa University, he has worked for and with the National Trust at local, regional and national level for more than thirty years. In 2013 he was awarded an OBE for services to heritage.

Samuel Pepys was born on 23 February 1633, the son of a London tailor. Pepys worked with the Navy Office, eventually rising to become Secretary of the Admiralty. He also became a JP, an MP and a Fellow of the Royal Society. In later life he was accused of being part of the anti-monarchist 'Popish Plot', and was twice imprisoned for it. Upon his second release he retired to Clapham, then considered to be 'in the country'. Samuel Pepys died on 26 May 1703. His diaries, which had been written in code, were bequeathed to Magdalen College, Cambridge, where they can still be viewed.

John Evelyn, born 31 October 1620, was a scholar, gardener, architect and diarist. Born in Surrey, Evelyn later settled in Deptford, London, and his diaries, like those of his friend and colleague Samuel Pepys, form a vivid account of life as a seventeenth-century courtier. Following the Great Fire, Evelyn submitted plans for the rebuilding of the city, and although these ultimately proved impossible to implement they brought him close to Christopher Wren and Charles II. He died in 1706.

ADRIAN TINNISWOOD

The Great Fire of London

VINTAGE

1 3 5 7 9 10 8 6 4 2

Vintage
20 Vauxhall Bridge Road,
London SW1V 2SA

Vintage Classics is part of the Penguin Random House
group of companies whose addresses can be found at
global.penguinrandomhouse.com.

Extracts from *By Permission of Heaven* copyright ©
Adrian Tinniswood 2003

The Great Fire of London in the Year of 1666: Private Collection / ©
Look and Learn / Peter Jackson Collection / Bridgeman Images

This edition first published by Vintage in 2016

www.vintage-books.co.uk

A CIP catalogue record for this book is available from the British Library

ISBN 9781784872144

Typeset in 11.5/13.75 pt Bembo
Jouve (UK), Milton Keynes
Printed and bound by Clays Ltd, St Ives plc

Penguin Random House is committed to a sustainable future
for our business, our readers and our planet. This book is made
from Forest Stewardship Council® certified paper.

CONTENTS

The GREAT FIRE of

ONDON in the Year 1666,

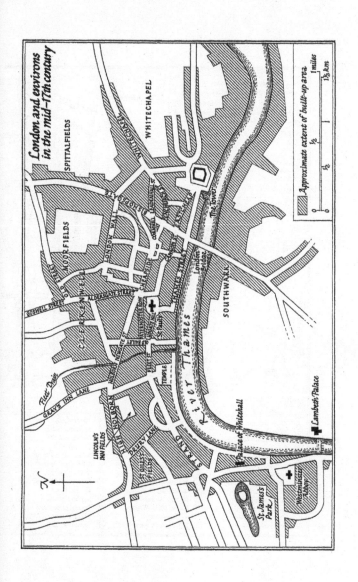

London and environs in the mid-17th century

SPITTALFIELDS

WHITECHAPEL

MOORFIELDS

CLERKENWELL

OLD STREET

GOSWELL STREET

ALDERSGATE STREET

LONDON WALL

BISHOPSGATE ST

THROGMORTON ST

CORNHILL

LEADENHALL ST

THREADNEEDLE ST

Exchange

St Paul's

WESTMINSTER

OLD BAILEY

NEWGATE ST

CHEAPSIDE

GRACECHURCH ST

FENCHURCH ST

The Tower

Fleet Ditch

GRAYS INN LANE

LINCOLN'S INN FIELDS

HIGH HOLBORN

DRURY LANE

ST GILES'S FIELDS

TEMPLE

STRAND

THAMES STREET

London Bridge

River Thames

SOUTHWARK

Palace of Whitehall

Lambeth Palace

St James's Park

Westminster Abbey

N

Approximate extent of built-up area

0   ½   1   miles
0   ½   1   1½ km

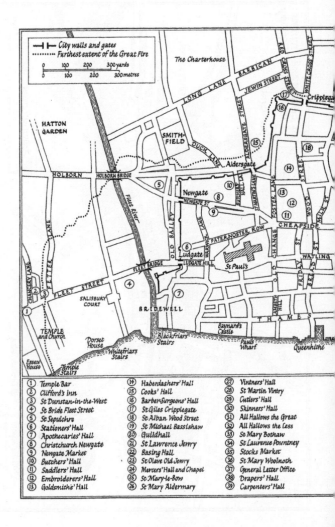

— City walls and gates	
.... Furthest extent of the Great Fire	

The Charterhouse

HATTON GARDEN

SMITHFIELD

HOLBORN HOLBORN BRIDGE

LONG LANE BARBICAN

JEWIN STREET

Cripplega

DUCK LANE

Aldersgate

Newgate

NEWGATE ST.

FETTER LANE

CHANCERY LANE

Fleet River

OLD BAILEY

PATERNOSTER ROW

CHEAPSIDE

POSTERN STREET

WOOD STREET

Ludgate

SALISBURY COURT

FLEET STREET

FLEET BRIDGE

LUDGATE HILL

St Pauls

WATLING

THAMES

TEMPLE and Church

BRIDEWELL

Baynard's Castle

Dorset House

Blackfriars Stairs

Pauls Wharf

Queenhithe

Essex House

Temple Stairs

Whitefriars Stairs

① Temple Bar
② Clifford's Inn
③ St Dunstan's-in-the-West
④ St Bride Fleet Street
⑤ St Sepulchre
⑥ Stationers' Hall
⑦ Apothecaries' Hall
⑧ Christchurch Newgate
⑨ Newgate Market
⑩ Butchers' Hall
⑪ Saddlers' Hall
⑫ Embroiderers' Hall
⑬ Goldsmiths' Hall

⑭ Haberdashers' Hall
⑮ Cooks' Hall
⑯ Barber-Surgeons' Hall
⑰ St Giles Cripplegate
⑱ St Alban Wood Street
⑲ St Michael Bassishaw
⑳ Guildhall
㉑ St Lawrence Jewry
㉒ Basing Hall
㉓ St Olave Old Jewry
㉔ Mercers' Hall and Chapel
㉕ St Mary-le-Bow
㉖ St Mary Aldermary

㉗ Vintners' Hall
㉘ St Martin Vintry
㉙ Cutlers' Hall
㉚ Skinners' Hall
㉛ All Hallows the Great
㉜ All Hallows the Less
㉝ St Mary Bothaw
㉞ St Laurence Pountney
㉟ Stocks Market
㊱ St Mary Woolnoth
㊲ General Letter Office
㊳ Drapers' Hall
㊴ Carpenters' Hall

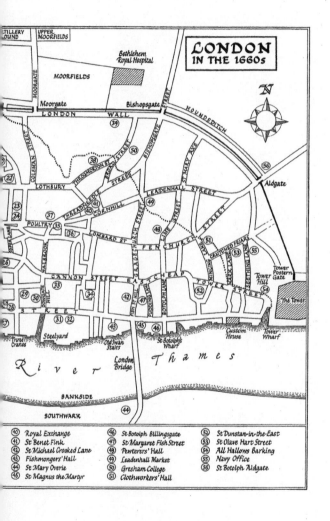

LONDON
IN THE 1660s

N

ARTILLERY GROUND

UPPER MOORFIELDS

Bethlehem Royal Hospital

MOORFIELDS

MOORGATE

Moorgate

Bishopsgate

LONDON WALL

HOUNDSDITCH

BISHOPSGATE

ST MARY AXE

Aldgate

㉒

LOTHBURY

THROGMORTON ST

BROAD STREET

LEADENHALL STREET

㉓
㉔
㉗
㊱
⑮

POULTRY

THREADNEEDLE ST

CORNHILL

LOMBARD ST

FENCHURCH STREET

CRUTCHED FRIARS

SEETHING LANE

Tower Hill

Tower Postern Gate

WALBROOK

CANNON STREET

EASTCHEAP

TOWER STREET

The Tower

Custom House

Tower Wharf

Three Cranes

Steelyard

Old Swan Stairs

St Botolph Wharf

London Bridge

River Thames

BANKSIDE

SOUTHWARK

㊹

㊵ Royal Exchange	㊻ St Botolph Billingsgate	㊼ St Dunstan-in-the-East
㊶ St Benet Fink	㊼ St Margaret Fish Street	㊽ St Olave Hart Street
㊷ St Michael Crooked Lane	㊽ Pewterers' Hall	㊾ All Hallows Barking
㊸ Fishmongers' Hall	㊾ Leadenhall Market	㊿ Navy Office
㊹ St Mary Overie	㊿ Gresham College	⑤⑥ St Botolph Aldgate
㊺ St Magnus the Martyr	㊿ Clothworkers' Hall	

Afterwards, everyone swore they had been expecting it. They pointed to the prophecies of doom and the Popish plots that had been the talk of the city all through that long, hot August. They reminded each other about the harbingers of calamity: the great pyramid of fire which had hovered ominously over the sea earlier in the year; the monster which had been born in a tenement slum just days before it happened – a terrible thing with a wolf's tail, a goat's breasts, the ears of a horse and a birthmark in the shape of a human face on its chest. Such portents were signs of God's wrath, people said. England had been called to account. England's debauched King had been shown the error of his ways.

But that was afterwards, when it was too late.

As dawn broke bright and clear on the first day of September 1666, no one dreamed they were waking to the last sunrise the old city would ever see. No one dreamed that over the next six days God would blot out the heavens, or that hell would break loose as fear and flame turned the streets of London into Armageddon.

1

THE FIRE BREAKS OUT

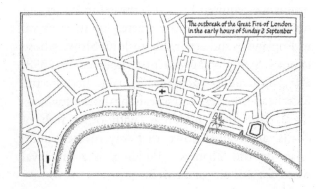

The outbreak of the Great Fire of London in the early hours of Sunday 2 September

Afterwards, Thomas Farriner was always quite clear about one thing. The events of that Saturday night were not his fault.

Farriner was an ordinary tradesman. His main source of income was a contract to produce ship's biscuit, an unleavened bread which was baked, sliced and then oven-dried. His client was the Navy's Victualling Office, which is why he was occasionally referred to in contemporary accounts of the Fire as 'the King's baker'; and his premises were on Pudding Lane, a narrow thoroughfare less than 100 yards long which ran north-to-south from the meat markets and butchers' stalls of Little Eastcheap down to Thames Street with its riverside wharves and warehouses. The parish church, St Margaret Fish Street, had been the site of a large fish market in the Middle Ages – a 1311 ordinance required French lampreys to be set out for sale under its walls immediately on their arrival in England – and according to John Stow, whose famous *Survey of London* first appeared in 1598, Pudding Lane had acquired its name because the Eastcheap butchers had a scalding-house for hogs there, 'and their puddings, with other filth of beasts, are voided down that way to their dung boats on the Thames'. 'Pudding' is a medieval word for entrails or bowels.

The area also had a more appetising reputation. Over the years, numbers of cooks and bakers had set up shop in and around Eastcheap, drawn there by the easy supply of fresh meat and the proximity of the Victualling Office near Little Tower Hill. Breads, pies and hot meats were all offered for sale to the public, and traders 'cried hot ribs of beef roasted, pies well baked, and other victuals'.

As well as baking hard tack for the navy, Farriner ran just such a business, making and selling bread (few households baked their own), and cooking both his own pies and pasties and those which had been prepared by his neighbours. His bakery was less than halfway up Pudding Lane; it lay behind the Star Inn on Fish Street, the main northern approach to London Bridge, which ran more or less parallel to the lane. He lived over the shop with his daughter Hanna, a maid and a manservant.

Thomas Farriner closed for business at the usual time on Saturday evening, around eight or nine at night. His oven was probably of the beehive type, a brick structure which was brought up to temperature by laying bundles of faggots directly on its floor and kindling them with a light from the bakehouse hearth. The faggots were raked out when the baker judged the oven to be hot enough; loaves were baked when it was at its hottest, and then as it cooled down their place was taken by pies and pasties.

So the oven should have been virtually cold by now. Thomas checked it and filled it with faggots ready for the morning. He prepared several pots of baked meat for Sunday dinner, raked up the coals in the hearth and went to bed. A couple of flitches of bacon were left beside the oven.

Hanna checked on the bakehouse around midnight, when she also took a last look round the house to make sure all was well. Then she too went to bed.

About an hour later the Farriners' manservant woke up. Smoke filled the ground floor of the bakery, and he could hardly breathe with the fumes. But he managed to climb the stairs and rouse Thomas, Hanna and the maid. Only now there was no way down, and the four found themselves trapped on the upper floor.

Someone, either Thomas or his manservant, hit on the idea of clambering out of one of the upstairs windows, crawling along the guttering and climbing back in through their neighbour's window. They were shouting as loud as they could to raise the alarm:

And now the doleful, dreadful, hideous Note
Of FIRE, is screem'd out with a deep-strain'd
   throat;
Horror, and fear, and sad distracted Cryes,
Chide Sloth away, and bids the Sluggard rise;
Most direful Exclamations are let fly
From every Tongue, Tears stand in every Eye.

At some point Hanna was badly burned. But she managed to scramble to safety along the eaves with her father. They were followed by the manservant. Only the maid was left in the house, too frightened of heights, or too confused by the noise and the smoke to escape. As the easterly gales whipped across the rooftops, she died there – the first victim of the Great Fire of London. No one even knows her name.

Like most London streets, the houses in Pudding Lane were timber-framed and linked so that two haphazard terraces faced each other, almost touching eaves in the centre of the lane where their upper storeys had been jettied out. People were hardly alert: the early hours of Sunday morning were a time when, as one contemporary put it, 'Slothfulness and the Heat of the Bed have riveted a Man to his Pillow, and made him almost incapable of waking, much less of acting and helping his Neighbours.' But community action was the normal and expected response to an accident of this sort, and the neighbours did stir themselves, roused by the Farriners' cries – and, in one case at least, by their abrupt arrival through a bedroom window. They threw on clothes and ran out into the street to see what was happening. Within minutes, there must have been dozens of anxious and bleary-eyed people milling around in the driving wind, shouting to make themselves heard over the crackling flames and using whatever came to hand to extinguish the blaze: buckets of water; shovelfuls of earth and dung; milk, beer and urine.

For nearly an hour, it looked as if the blaze could easily be confined to the bakery, with minor damage to the homes on either side. As a precaution, neighbours began to bundle up their valuables and drag them out into the street; the summer had been extraordinarily hot and there had been little rain, so that the timber and plaster were very dry, and the wind was obviously fanning the flames. The parish constables arrived, and decided that the situation warranted the presence of the Lord Mayor. As chief magistrate of the City it was Sir Thomas Bludworth's job to authorise any radical measures involving citizens' property; and the constables, uneasy at the speed with which the flames were consuming Farriner's bakery, were looking for permission to override the wishes of neighbours and pull down buildings in the street, so as to prevent the spread of the fire.

But Bludworth, whose success in City politics was due to his Royalist sympathies rather than any innate ability, was a weak man. Although he was coming to the end of his year in office, he didn't have the experience, the leadership skills or the natural authority to take command of the situation. True, he was prompt to arrive on the scene; but what he saw there – the raging fire, the chaos and confusion and heat and noise that always accompany such accidents – terrified him.

As the fire moved from the bakery to the adjoining houses, creeping along the lane towards the warehouses of Thames Street, more level-headed men among the firefighters wanted to form firebreaks by demolishing several untouched houses. But Bludworth simply said that he dared not do it without the consent of the owners. Most of the shops and homes were rented, so those owners were God knew where. Not in Pudding Lane, for sure.

Pressed to reconsider, Sir Thomas took refuge in bluster. The fire wasn't all that serious, he said. 'A woman could piss it out.' And with that he went home to bed and a place in the history books.

Bludworth wasn't alone. In Seething Lane, seven streets away, Samuel and Elizabeth Pepys were woken abruptly at 3 a.m. by their favourite maid, Jane Birch. The servants had stayed up late to prepare for the dinner which the couple were giving that day; as Jane was going to bed she happened to look out of her window and catch sight of an unmistakable glow in the west. As soon as she told him that there was a fire, Samuel leaped out of bed, threw on his dressing-gown and followed Jane to her chamber. The blaze seemed close – just beyond the next street, in fact. But sights like that were not uncommon, and Samuel decided there

7

was nothing to worry about. Like Sir Thomas Bludworth, he shrugged and went back to bed.

When he got up four hours later, the fire seemed further away. He also thought, presumably because the daylight took away from the drama, that it was 'not so much as it was'. Jane soon disabused him; she had heard that 'above 300 houses have been burned down tonight by the fire we saw, and that it was now burning down all Fishstreet by London Bridge'.

Feeling anxious, Samuel left the Navy Office in Seething Lane and walked the hundred yards or so to the Tower of London. The Lieutenant of the Tower, Alderman Sir John Robinson, was an old acquaintance (although not a friend – Pepys thought him a fool, a glutton and 'a talking bragging Bufflehead'); and accompanied by Robinson's little son, he climbed to the battlements and surveyed the scene.

What he saw appalled him. Thanks to Bludworth, an ordinary house-fire had turned into a street-fire; and that street-fire now threatened to engulf the entire south-eastern corner of the City. During the night the easterly gale carried sparks and burning embers from the bakery across into Fish Street, where they ignited hay in the yard of the Star Inn. The trail of destruction had crept down Fish Street Hill, destroying St Margaret's and the neighbouring church of St Magnus the Martyr, which had presided over the northern end of London Bridge since before the Norman Conquest. Worse, it had reached Thames Street, where it found the wharves and met 'nothing but old paper buildings and the most combustible matter of Tarr, Pitch, Hemp, Rosen, and Flax which was all layd up thereabouts'. Now the houses which lined the bridge itself were in flames.

Pepys spent a few moments talking to Sir John, who told him where the fire had started and how fast it was moving. Then he decided to see for himself at close quarters, and hired a boat to take him upriver, through the piers of the bridge.

What Samuel saw was worse – much worse – than the prospect of smoke and flames and burning streets that the battlements of the Tower had offered. About a quarter of a mile of the north bank of the river was on fire. Lighters and small boats were clustering round the stairs at Old Swan Lane beside the bridge while everyone in the neighbourhood frantically tried to save their goods from the flames which marched from house to house, and street to street. They threw their belongings into the waiting boats or, if there were no boats at hand, into the river itself. As the fire took hold, the pigeons which Londoners kept for food fluttered over their burning homes, hovering at balconies and windows until the flames singed their wings and they fluttered down to their deaths.

As Pepys watched, flames suddenly appeared at the very top of the steeple of St Laurence Pountney, one of the tallest landmarks in this part of the City. The fire 'appearing first at the top discovered itself with so much terror, as if taking a view from that lofty place of what it intended to devour'. Within minutes it had caught hold, and the burning spire toppled over and crashed down into the street.

Pepys decided he had to get to Whitehall. He must see the King.

2

THE FIRE GOES UNCHECKED

In a society where most houses were timber-framed, in an age when every home had several open fires and every chamber was lit by naked flame, house-fires were not unusual. Like anyone else, Londoners sometimes set candles under shelves, or left them burning near their beds when they fell asleep, or neglected to fix them securely in their candlesticks; they used rush lights to peer under beds for chamber pots, and aired their clothes by hanging them too close to the fire, and put hot pots and pans on flammable surfaces. Even the King himself was not immune to danger. There was a minor blaze at Whitehall in 1661; another in 1662, when a gale caused the Palace to catch fire four times in a single night; and yet another – this time in the lodgings of the King's mistress, the Countess of Castlemaine – in January 1664.

Nor was it that unusual for a fire to consume

streets or even entire districts before it was finally brought under control. Over the course of the seventeenth century, English towns suffered at least twenty major disasters in which fire destroyed more than one hundred houses. In August 1613, for example, around half of Dorchester, the county town of Dorset, was burned to the ground after a chandler accidentally set light to some tallow. The previous year Tiverton in Devon had been laid waste by fire; in 1628 a third of the houses in Banbury, Northamptonshire, were destroyed by flames; in October 1644, 300 houses in Oxford. Like the fire in Farriner's bakery, the disasters at Tiverton, Banbury and Oxford all began on a Sunday, affording Puritan preachers plenty of scope for speculation on wickedness and divine wrath.

The capital, though, had known nothing on this scale since 1212, when fire devastated housing north and south of London Bridge and trapped a large number of people on the bridge itself. (According to one account,★ thousands were killed – four

★ 'Three thousand bodies, some half-burnt, were found in the river Thames: besides those who perished altogether by fire. It broke out on the south side of the Bridge. Multitudes of people rushed to the rescue of the inhabitants of houses on the bridge, and while thus engaged the fire broke out on the north side also, and hemmed them in, making a holocaust of those who were not killed by leaping into the Thames' (John Timbs, *Curiosities of London* [n.d.], 340).

centuries later the disaster was still known as 'the Great Fire of London'.) But it had seen its fair share of smaller fires, the most serious of which occurred in February 1633, when a servant left a bucket of hot ashes underneath a staircase in one of the houses at the northern end of London Bridge. The resulting blaze spread up Fish Street Hill and destroyed around eighty buildings in the parish of St Magnus the Martyr.

Fatalities were often surprisingly low. An old woman named Cicely Bingham was the only casualty in the 1613 fire that left Jacobean Dorchester 'a heap of ashes for travellers to sigh at'. And when a house in Lothbury – then fast becoming a wealthy merchant quarter of the City – burned to the ground in December 1662, people thought it remarkable that all seven occupants (one of whom was the daughter of the current Lord Mayor) were killed, 'not one thing, dog nor cat, escaping; nor any of the neighbours almost hearing of it till the house was quite down and burnt. How this should come to pass, God knows, but a most strange thing it is!'

There was no fire brigade to call, no police. No emergency services at all, in fact. But there were still procedures for dealing with fires and, if they seemed haphazard, even chaotic, they were usually effective.

So when fire broke out in the City, several things were supposed to happen. The alarm was raised in the street and adjoining homes were evacuated, their occupants grabbing their most precious possessions and bundling them up or, if the fire was moving fast, simply throwing them out of doors and windows. The church bells were 'rung backwards' – that is, with a muffled peal – to call public-spirited citizens to action; and the parish constables and other responsible figures moved quickly to block off both ends of the affected street, 'that the rude people may be kept from doing mischief for sometime they do more harm than fire'.

In theory, all streets and lanes leading to the Thames were to be manned by double rows of firefighters, with one human chain passing empty buckets down to the river, and the other passing full buckets back up to the fire. Anyone on higher ground was supposed to throw down water as quickly as they could in the hope that it would run towards the site of the fire, where those on the front line could sweep it towards the flames.

The supply of water was crucial. There were waterwheels under the northern end of London Bridge, installed in 1581 by a Dutchman, Pieter Morice. When the tide was right they pumped water up to a tower at Cornhill, the highest point in the City; from there a system of elm pipes and lead quills supplied the houses round about. (Morice apparently demonstrated how effective his system was by shooting a jet of water right over the tower of St Magnus the Martyr.) And in 1609 the New River Company had established a reservoir in Islington, bringing in spring water from Hertfordshire, thirty-eight miles away. The Islington Water House, as it was known, supplied around 30,000 homes in the City through its network of pipes. In the event of a fire it was often possible to open a pipe next to the house that was burning, and either plug a second pipe into it like a hose, to play on the flames, or use it to fill buckets.

The bucket wasn't the only piece of equipment available. Most parishes kept long ladders in their church towers specifically for use in fighting fires. These towers also often housed at least one fire-hook – a heavy pole, perhaps thirty feet long, which needed two or three men to carry and manoeuvre it. (It was sometimes mounted on a wheeled carriage rather like a bier.) There was a sturdy iron hook and ring at one end, and a second ring fixed halfway down. The idea was to use the hook like a grappling iron to grab the timber frame of a burning building or its neigh-bour downwind; then, using ropes attached to the two rings, firefighters could pull the building down.

Many parishes also carried scoops – iron shovels that were used to scoop water or earth and hurl it over the fire – and squirts. A squirt was shaped like a big syringe with two handles. Made of brass or wood, it held four pints of water, and needed two or three men to work it. (A modern diesel pump supplied from a hydrant delivers more than 33 gallons per second, thus depositing those 4 pints of water onto a fire in 0.015 of a second.) Its nozzle was dunked into a pond, or a tub of water, and the piston was pulled out; then it was pointed at the fire and the piston was pushed in. More sophisticated models were mounted on frames and pivoted, so that they could be dipped into the water and then pointed up at the fire more easily: they were used in London as early as 1584, when, decked with garlands, they led the Lord Mayor's procession to Westminster and squirted water into the crowd, forcing it to give way.

The City authorities advised that 'every parish should have hooks ladders squirts buckets and scoops in readiness on every occasion'. But the most impressive weapon in the Restoration firefighter's armoury was a more elaborate and more recent invention – the carriage-mounted pump, or fire engine.

The fire engine first arrived in England in about 1625, when Roger Jones was granted a patent to produce an 'Engine or Instrument artificiallie wrought with scrues and other devices made of Copper or brasse or other metall for the casting of water'. The idea had surfaced in Nuremberg a decade or so earlier, and the first English engine was much the same as its German counterpart: a single-acting force pump with a vertical cylinder, connected to a short delivery pipe made of brass. (Hoses of canvas or leather didn't appear until 1690.) The pump was worked by long handles at the front and back of the engine, and the whole thing was fixed to a strong enclosed frame – which doubled as a water reservoir – and was mounted on a wheelless sled. The patent claimed that ten men working the engine could quench a fire with more ease and speed than 500 using buckets and ladders, thus saving lives and preserving property which would otherwise have to be pulled down to prevent the spread of the flames.

Roger Jones died of plague within months of the patent being granted, and a Lothbury founder named William Burroughs took up the idea; between the late 1620s and the early 1660s Burroughs made about sixty engines 'for City and Country', at a price of £35 each. They were used at the London Bridge fire of 1633, and again four

years later in a blaze at the Earl of Arundel's house
on the Strand. As a result the Lord Mayor was
urged to see that 'the great parishes should provide
themselves with engines and the lesser ones should
join together in providing them'; and in 1642 he
asked each of the major City Companies to supply
a fire engine for the public good. At least two –
the Goldsmiths and the Ironmongers – obliged.
A few years later the lawyers of both the Inner
Temple and the Middle Temple had engines of
their own, and several were also kept in Scotland
Yard, ready to fight a serious fire in the Palace
of Whitehall. The best was generally reckoned to
be the engine kept in the church of St James
Clerkenwell, conveniently near to the New River
Company's Water House and reservoirs; it was
run a close second by a newer engine at St Bride
Fleet Street.

So with all this equipment, all these procedures and
preparations for managing disaster, what went
wrong? Because it was clear by mid-morning on
Sunday that things *had* gone wrong, very wrong
indeed; a small fire in a baker's shop had already
turned into something more frightening. Sir Edward
Atkyns, a lawyer living at Lincoln's Inn to the west
of the City boundary, was in church when his
devotions were interrupted by shouting in the street

outside; the story of how the spire of St Laurence Pountney mysteriously caught fire before the flames in Pudding Lane reached it had spread to the Inns of Court, and people were running up and down, screaming that the Dutch and the French 'were in armes, & had fired ye Citty'.

The minister immediately abandoned his service and dismissed the congregation, but Atkyns decided that he was so far from the centre of trouble that there was really nothing to worry about. Further off still, young William Taswell was listening to a sermon in Westminster Abbey when he became aware of a commotion outside. People were running about 'in a seeming disquietude and consternation'. Someone yelled that London was burning; the cry was taken up by others; and Taswell immediately forgot the preacher and dashed out of the Abbey, down to Parliament Steps, where 'I soon perceived four boats crowded with objects of distress. These had escaped from the fire scarce under any covering except that of a blanket.'

The fire engines obviously hadn't helped much in Pudding Lane or down by the wharves on Thames Street. But, judging from contemporary accounts, they were more used to travelling hopefully than arriving. The three engines brought up to combat the London Bridge fire of 1633 had

had no impact: 'they were all broken for the tide was very low that they c^d get no water – and the pipes which were cut yielded but little'. And although at the Arundel House fire in 1637 'the good use of the engines for spouting water manifestly appeared', they didn't actually make any difference, because they were so cumbersome and had to come from so far away that none of them arrived until it was too late.

History repeated itself in Pudding Lane. Massively heavy and fixed on sleds, each engine required twenty-eight men or a team of eight horses to move it. Very few streets were paved; most were cobbled, and so narrow that any obstruction – a cart, a crowd – brought progress to an abrupt halt. Even at the best of times, traffic jams were commonplace and entire districts were often brought to a gridlocked standstill for hours at a time. This morning, with panic mounting and hundreds of households on the move all along Thames Street, the task of manoeuvring these leviathans through the lanes and alleys around Fish Street was well-nigh impossible.

By the time the engines *did* arrive, the flames were so fierce that without any delivery hoses they couldn't get close enough to the seat of the fire to be of any use. In fact they couldn't even get into Pudding Lane – it was so narrow that firefighters were unable to maintain a safe distance from the buildings on the western side, where Farriner's bakery lay. Even if they had, the water-wheels under London Bridge were burning, so the water supply for that part of the City had dried up. As gangs of men tried desperately to manoeuvre right up to the river bank so that they could fill their reservoirs, several pumps were lost, including the famous Clerkenwell fire engine, which had been dragged right across the City only to topple into the Thames.

But it wasn't just the engines' failure to perform which allowed the fire to spread so dramatically. The easterly gales of Saturday night were still blowing hard across south-east England: 'the fire gets mastery, and burns dreadfully; and God with his great bellows blows upon it'. Coupled with the effects of the long, tinder-dry summer and the failure of the water supply, the efficiency with which God's bellows fanned the flames took everyone by surprise. And Bludworth's failure of nerve was crucial. As the sun rose on Sunday morning, he could still have authorised the demolition of houses in Fish Street and Pudding Lane. If he had, the history of London would have been quite different.

Fresh from watching the collapse of St Laurence Pountney, Pepys reached Whitehall and went straight to the Chapel Royal, a few yards from his landing place at Whitehall Stairs. Courtiers crowded round him as he told of the chaos he had seen along Thames Street; within minutes the King had been informed and Pepys was brought before him and the Duke of York. Both men were 'much troubled' by the news. Charles expressly told Pepys to go back to Bludworth and command him to begin pulling down houses; James said that the Life Guards, many of whom were billeted in and around Whitehall, were available to help fight the fire if the Mayor wanted them. Secretary of State Lord Arlington repeated this offer to him as he was leaving, 'as a great secret'. The ordering of troops into the City was a sensitive issue.

Pepys borrowed a coach to take him back into the City. It got as far as St Paul's Cathedral before the crowded streets forced him to walk. Organised attempts to put out the fire had been all but abandoned; everyone was frantic to save themselves and their goods. They carried their possessions on wagons, in handcarts, on their backs. The sick were hauled through the crowded streets, still in their beds. Those of the City's 109 parish churches which were not directly threatened were filling rapidly – not with Sunday worshippers, but with furniture and valuables, as merchants, tradesmen and ordinary householders turned them into warehouses.

Pepys found Bludworth in Cannon Street, between St Paul's and the river. The Mayor was distracted by the effort of trying – and failing – to coordinate the firefighting operation. With a handkerchief round his neck he was close to collapse, 'like a fainting woman'. His response to the King's message was to cry, 'Lord, what can I do? I am spent! People will not obey me. I have been pulling down houses. But the fire overtakes us faster then we can do it.' But anxious to retain some semblance of dignity and civic authority, he was reluctant to take up the Duke of York's offer of soldiers; there was no need for that, he said. And he was exhausted: he needed to go home. So he did.

Pepys also went home. It was now midday, and he got back to Seething Lane to find his dinner guests waiting for him.

All things considered, the meal wasn't quite the disaster it might have been. True, it was interrupted at one point by the arrival of a neighbour looking for news of mutual friends whose Fish Street homes had been destroyed early that morning. But on the positive side, Barbara Sheldon's new husband William seemed a decent enough chap; and if circumstances made it inappropriate for Pepys to show off his new closet to Mr Moone, at least 'we had an extraordinary good dinner, and as merry as at this time we could be'.

But the party quickly broke up; and Pepys walked Moone back to St Paul's. The eastern end of Cannon Street was on fire now, and the rapid spread of the flames was continuing to take people by surprise. Goods were evacuated to 'safe' houses which were streets away from the flames, only to be moved again and again as the fire came closer.

At some point in the afternoon Sir Edward Atkyns wandered out of his Lincoln's Inn lodgings and into the Temple Garden. He wasn't as sanguine as he had been that morning: the distance between the fire and the Inns of Court was noticeably decreased. 'The wind being high,' he wrote to his brother, 'it grew very formidable, and wee began to thinke of its nearer approach.' Great flakes of flame were blowing everywhere, stinging the face and burning the clothes. As far away as Westminster, William Taswell could see them flash up into the air and fly for hundreds of yards before they landed 'and uniting themselves to various dry substances, set on fire houses very remote from each other in point of situation'.

The King sailed down from Whitehall with the Duke in the royal barge to view the destruction. Both men were convinced that demolishing houses to isolate the fire was the only possible way to prevent its spread. And in spite of Bludworth's protestations, that still wasn't happening.

They disembarked at Queenhithe, the old quay on Thames Street which was now on the front line of the firefighting operations, and called not for Bludworth but for Alderman Sir Richard Browne. Browne had been both Lord Mayor and an MP for the City in the past; but more importantly, he had a great reputation in London as a military leader, directing trained bands during the Civil War and, during his Mayoralty in 1661, commanding the operation which had put down Thomas Venner's Fifth Monarchist rising.

In a risky move which showed how seriously he viewed the situation, Charles overrode the Lord Mayor's authority as chief magistrate and told Browne to pull down buildings, concentrating on the area below London Bridge towards the Tower, where the presence of large quantities of gunpowder was making everyone nervous. He also ignored Bludworth's refusal to ask for troops. The sixty-year-old Earl of Craven, a Lord Mayor's son and a professional soldier with a string of battle honours stretching back to service with Maurice of Orange in the early 1620s, was ordered into the City with his regiment of Coldstream Guards 'to be more particularly assisting to the Lord Mayor and Magistrates . . . [and] to be helpful by what ways they could in so great a calamity'.

The King and the Duke hoped to contain the

fire along the waterfront by halting its slow spread eastward at St Botolph's Wharf, which lay between Pudding Lane and the Tower; and making a stand against its much faster westward movement at Three Cranes Stairs, a public landing stage about 600 yards upriver. But though the wharves and storehouses along Thames Street had initially fuelled the fire, for the most part confining its spread to the waterfront, the wind was now veering erratically both north and south, pushing the flames up into the centre of the City in a broad, bow-shaped arc. They snaked up to the top of Fish Street Hill, through the meat markets of Eastcheap and along into Cannon Street. 'The time of London's fall is come; the fire hath received its commission from God to burn down the city, and therefore all attempts to hinder it are in vain.'

As dusk came on, the moonlit sky over the south-eastern quarter of the City remained bright and yellow, 'in a most horrid malicious bloody flame, not like the fine flame of an ordinary fire'. The blaze seemed to acquire a malevolent life of its own: no matter what men did to extinguish it, it imme-diately recovered. 'It leaps, and mounts, and makes the more furious onset, drives back its opposers, snatcheth their weapons out of their hands, seizeth upon the water-houses and engines, burns them, spoils them, and makes them unfit for service.'

In the eighteen hours or so since the fire had broken out at Farriner's, it had destroyed twenty-two alleys and wharves, nearly a thousand homes and shops, and six Livery Company Halls, including those of the Vintners, the Watermen and the powerful Fishmongers, whose Hall had been bequeathed to the Company in 1434. Nine churches were in ruins along with the parishes they served: as well as St Margaret Fish Street, St Magnus the Martyr and St Laurence Pountney, St Botolph Billingsgate had gone. So had All Hallows the Great and All Hallows the Less, two medieval churches which stood almost side by side just south of a section of Thames Street known as the Ropery, because ropes were traditionally made and sold in the high street there. They were also just north of one of the City's biggest hay wharves, a fact which ensured their destruction. Other casualties were St Mary Bothaw, where London's first mayor, Henry Fitz Ailwyn, was buried in 1212; St Martin Vintry, 'beautifully glazed' in the fifteenth century, according to Stow; and St Michael Crooked Lane, the last resting place of another famous Lord Mayor – William Walworth, who preferred to stab rebel leader Wat Tyler rather than negotiate with him and thus brought the Peasants' Revolt of 1381 to an abrupt end. Of those nine churches, six were lost for ever: only All Hallows the Great, St Magnus and St Michael would be rebuilt. No one knew it then, of course, but already London was irrevocably changed.

During the evening, the well-to-do whose homes and livelihoods were not directly affected began to gather across the river in Southwark. They listened to the roars and groans as buildings tumbled. They watched the pyrotechnics lighting up the night sky and eating into the metropolis.

Pepys, who had gone back to Whitehall in the afternoon, met up with his wife in St James's Park, and together they took a boat downriver, ending up in an alehouse on Bankside, just across from Three Cranes Stairs. As the darkness grew, through the smoke they could make out burning steeples and rivulets of flame which criss-crossed the City until they met in one massive arch of fire a mile long.

Samuel broke down and cried for his city.

3

THE RUMOUR MILL

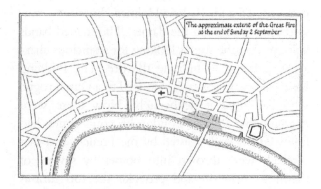

'The approximate extent of the Great Fire at the end of Sunday 2 September'

The Earl of Clarendon later pinpointed Monday morning as the time when almost everybody began to suspect that the disaster was no accident. The day produced 'first a jealousy,' he wrote, 'and then an universal conclusion, that this fire came not by chance'.

In fact, suspicions had already been roused the previous day. For two or three hours on Sunday afternoon Thomas Middleton, a surgeon living in the parish of St Bride Fleet Street, had stood at the top of a church steeple near the Three Cranes and watched as fire broke out in one house, then another and another some distance away. 'These and such like observations begat in me a persuasion that the fire was maintained by design,' he said; and by that evening the theory that Sir Edward Atkyns had heard in church – that the Dutch had struck back in revenge for Sir Robert Holmes's bonfire* – was spreading faster than the flames. The trained bands were out on the streets looking for suspicious characters rather than fighting the fire. The Pudding Lane bakery, it was said, belonged to a Dutch rogue who had fired it deliberately. Now there were rumours that all over London his countrymen had followed his lead, assisted by the French, and that 'fireballs were thrown into houses by several of them, to help on and provoke the too furious flames'. This in itself was enough to provoke a wave of xenophobic violence. William Taswell saw a mob looting the shop of a French painter: the rioters stripped it bare and then levelled it to the ground, on the pretence of foiling any attempt the proprietor might have made to fire it and thus add to the general conflagration. William also watched appalled as a blacksmith walked up to an

---

* The name given by the English to a raid a few weeks earlier in which the swashbuckling Sir Robert Holmes set fire to the Dutch town of West-Terschelling.

unsuspecting Frenchman in the street and hit him across the head with an iron bar. More than three decades later he could still remember how the poor man fell, how his blood flowed 'in a plentiful stream down to his ancles'.

There are no reliable estimates for the number of foreigners living in London and its suburbs in 1666, but they certainly ran into thousands. There were various diplomats and ambassadors, of course: a Swedish embassy consisting of 124 people had arrived at the end of June, and its members were currently lodged at various places to the west of the City, including Covent Garden and Lincoln's Inn. But the vast majority of aliens had made London their home. In spite of the war, many were French or Dutch Protestants, asylum seekers who had arrived in England in the wake of religious persecutions in Europe; most were skilled artisans. At the end of the sixteenth century a return of aliens in the City, Southwark and Westminster claimed that there were 5,141. In 1639 the Privy Council ordered another census of foreigners in Westminster and the City; this reported the presence of 1,668 aliens, divided pretty evenly between the two districts. In Westminster there were 641 French and 176 Dutch, along with 15 Italians and 6 Spaniards; they were in the main painters, picture-drawers, engravers, musicians and silver-workers.

One in four of the aliens resident in the City itself was a weaver. There was a large Walloon contingent – 303 out of a total of 830 – and many of these were presumably refugees from the Spanish Netherlands who had settled in London during the Thirty Years War. But there were also 228 French and 221 Dutch, 24 Germans, 11 Italians, 2 Poles and a Bohemian, a Norwegian, a Savoyard, a Venetian, a Bavarian from the Palatinate, a Florentine and a Hamburger.

Periodically during the first half of the seventeenth century the Weavers' Company expressed concern that foreigners were taking work from their own members, so that 'our own people are grown into the most extreme wants, and know not what to do in winter-time when work will fail and be more scant'. And in the months after the Restoration, resentment surfaced in a depressingly familiar way at the 'multitude of French now in town, who eat the bread out of the mouths of natives', with MPs claiming, most improbably, that 35,000 French silk weavers had arrived in London over the previous three years.★

★ Around the same time the Lord Mayor and aldermen also complained directly to the King of 'the great increase of the Jews in the City, [and] their interference with the trade of the Citizens', and urged their expulsion from the kingdom. Nothing was done; and, interestingly, there is no record of any anti-Semitic attacks in the aftermath of the Fire.

The London weavers weren't the only group to complain about foreign incursions into their territory. Early in 1662, journeymen feltmakers successfully petitioned for a change in local laws which would bar their employers from taking on foreign workers. And at various points in Charles II's reign, London's carpenters, tailors and fish-mongers all complained that they were being impoverished by competition from foreign nationals resident in the capital.

A nasty strain of xenophobia already ran deep in the hearts of many Londoners. In Elizabethan times, European guidebooks warned the unwary traveller that the English were very suspicious of foreigners. A century later that attitude was confirmed by John Evelyn. In his *A Character of England* (1659), which purported to be a letter home written by a French visitor, he described how

Arriv'd at the Metropolis of civility, London, . . . we put ourselves in Coach with some persons of quality, who came to conduct us to our Lodging; but neither was this passage without honours done to us, the kennel dirt, squibs, roots and ramshornes being favours which were frequently cast at us by the children, and apprentices without reproofe; civilities, that in Paris, a Gentleman as seldome meets withall . . . You would imagine

your self amongst a Legion of Devills, and in the
suburb of Hell.

Evelyn's view of the reception given to foreign
visitors in London is echoed by Pepys, who
commented on how his fellow citizens laughed
and jeered the arrival in 1662 of an embassy from
Russia; and also by Samuel Sorbière, who found
the following year that not only were the English
haughty towards strangers, but that little boys
routinely chased after him in the street crying,
'French dog! French dog!'

Identifiable by their dress, their manners, their
accents, their names, foreigners were easy targets
for the fear and anger which were spreading from
street to street faster than the flames themselves
that Monday. The government took steps to
prevent terrorists from fleeing the country: Lord
Arlington wrote to the governor of the forts at
Gravesend, ordering him to prevent all shipping
leaving. He also told the authorities at Dover to
place an embargo on all vessels and persons
attempting to get out of the Cinque Ports.

One of the first foreigners to be arrested was
Cornelius Rietvelt, a Dutch baker with a shop in
Westminster. The conjunction of Dutchmen and
bakeries proved too much for his neighbours. On

Sunday evening or early Monday morning he was accused of attempting to fire his premises, stripped of all he possessed and finally committed to Westminster's notorious Gatehouse Prison, of which a previous occupant, Richard Lovelace, had written 'Stone walls do not a prison make / Nor iron bars a cage'. In Rietvelt's case they did.

News and rumour travelled fast. At ten o'clock on Monday morning a distraught Anne Hobart was writing from her home in Chancery Lane to tell her cousin in the country that the fire had begun in a Dutch baker's house in Pudding Lane. Lady Hobart, who was frantically trying to organise the evacuation of her household, was in no doubt as to the cause of the disaster: ''Tis the Duch fire,' she wrote. She also knew of Rietvelt's arrest. 'Thar was one tacken in Westminster seting his outhous on fier & thay have attempted to fier many plases & thar is a bundanc tacken with granades & pouder, Castell yard* was set on fier, i am all most out of my wits . . . O pray for us . . . O pety me.'

Monday also saw the arrest of a maid, Anne English, who lived in Covent Garden. Five witnesses claimed they had heard Anne say that a group of Frenchmen had recently visited her

---

* Baynard's Castle, on the north bank of the Thames at Blackfriars.

master's house and advised him to move his goods, 'for within six weeks that house and all the street would be burned down to the ground'. She was taken for interrogation to Whitehall, where she denied saying any such thing. She insisted all she had done was to mention in company that 'she had heard that the French and Dutch had kindled the fire in the city'. Presumably her story was believed, since nothing more is heard of her.

Others weren't so lucky. All through Monday the mob grew more violent – and more irrational. In Newgate Market they beat up a member of the Portuguese Ambassador's household, claiming he had been caught in the act of throwing a fireball into a house which had subsequently burst into flames. He told the justices who interrogated him that he had been walking along the street when he saw a crust of bread on the ground; he put it on a window sill, a common Portuguese custom. The bread was found exactly where he said he had left it – two doors down from the house which was burning – but like many foreigners he was sent to gaol anyway, for his own safety, and quietly released a day or so later. A Frenchman was rescued by four Life Guards, who found him being beaten in the street by a gang that claimed they had caught him in the act of firebombing a house. That afternoon the surgeon Thomas Middleton, who had spent

Sunday night at home in St Bride's only to be drawn back to the City, was passing a tobacco merchant's house in Watling Street when a youth was unceremoniously thrown out into the road at his feet. Middleton thought the young man looked suspicious – 'he seemed to be a Frenchman' – so he grabbed hold of him, only to find a powder horn under his coat. Just as sinister, the lad spoke with an accent and carried a book called *The Jewish Government*. He claimed the tobacco merchant knew him, but the merchant flatly denied it; and with the help of a parish constable Middleton dragged him off to the house of correction at Old Bridewell. They only just managed to reach the gaol: angry crowds jeered the 'French rascal' as they passed and, according to the surgeon, were more than ready to kill the hapless suspect. He was placed in solitary confinement until a magistrate could interrogate him.

Bridewell burned down the next day.

4

ATTEMPTS TO HALT THE FIRE

Throughout Monday, sporadic efforts were still being made to halt the spread of the flames. They were often courageous and dogged, but there was little attempt to mount a City-wide operation. Contemporary accounts make no mention of Bludworth, whose responsibility it was to coordinate the firefighting. We can only assume that, like most of his fellow citizens, he decided that discretion and self-interest were the better parts of valour, and ran for cover.

While William Taswell's father was intent on saving his possessions in Bear Lane – and being robbed in the process – the boy himself was more altruistically engaged. Despite the fire, William had gone to lessons as usual on Monday morning. Now John Dolben, the Dean of Westminster, marched the school on foot right into the heart of the City, determined 'to put a stop if possible to the conflagration'. They forced their way through the crowded streets until they reached St Dunstan-in-the-East, 'a fair and large church of an ancient building' which stood between Thames Street and Tower Street, not far from the Custom House. St Dunstan was only a couple of hundred yards away from Pudding Lane but, because the gales continued to push the fire west and north and the eastward creep was much less dramatic, it was still on the boundary of Monday's fire zone. But it had caught nevertheless, and for hours on end the Westminster boys fetched water while young Taswell acted as page to Dolben, running errands and taking messages. They eventually put out the flames; and after this small but significant victory, Dolben duly led his troops back to Westminster.

St Dunstan burned down early the following morning.

Heroic as they were, efforts like that of Dolben and his boys were doomed to fail in the absence of an organised operation. Indeed, where parish-based firefighting was still going on it was so haphazard that it did more harm than good. Buildings may have been pulled down with hooks in the prescribed manner; but no one thought to clear the timbers – indeed, where could they have taken them? – so the flames managed to cross even the widest streets and open spaces, leapfrogging from pyre to pyre.

As 'the spreading Flames now conquer all they meet / And walk in Triumph through the frighted streets', attempts to quell the fire seemed to have ceased entirely. On Monday night Evelyn watched the Thames covered with barges and boats, and straggling caravans of carts and pedestrians making their way out of the City gates towards the open fields to the north and east, where makeshift tents and encampments were springing up everywhere. 'Scarcely a back either of man or woman that hath strength, but had a burden on it in the streets,' wrote Thomas Vincent.

Not one to worry too much about accurate figures, Evelyn reckoned that there were 10,000 houses on fire, beneath a pall of smoke 56 miles long. The true figures weren't quite so dramatic, but they were bad enough. On Monday alone, thirty-nine more parishes had been destroyed as the fire scythed through mansions and hovels alike. The Livery Companies lost another eight Halls, including the brand new Hall in Cloak Lane which the Cutlers had only just finished paying for, and the ancient Hall and chapel of the Mercers at the eastern end of Cheapside, which was destroyed late on Monday night. About

1,500 yards of waterfront were burned: the stairs at Queenhithe, where the King and the Duke of York had surveyed the devastation and consulted with Sir Richard Browne the previous afternoon, had gone; so had Baynard's Castle at Blackfriars, home to Catherine of Aragon and Anne Boleyn, and the place where both Lady Jane Grey and Mary Tudor were proclaimed Queen of England.

Over the past twenty-four hours the great arc of devastation had spread out north and west from the original fire zone until it covered several hundred acres. It snaked through the alleys and roared through the broader streets, moving down Cornhill in the night, burning the Stocks Market and breaking into Cheapside.

There was no darkness: the fire shone with such a bright light that it was as though it was noon. Evelyn thought the City was being engulfed in a firestorm. 'The noise and cracking and thunder of the impetuous flames, the shrieking of women and children, the hurry of people, the fall of Towers, Houses and Churches, was like an hideous storme, and the aire all about so hot and inflam'd that at the last one was not able to approach it.' Worse still, those impetuous flames were creeping eastward, against the prevailing winds – and towards the Tower of London, home of the Ordnance Office and its considerable stores of gunpowder. John, Lord Berkeley, an Ordnance Commissioner and a member of the Duke of York's household, sent a rather desperate note from the Tower to the Navy Office, begging that all available fire engines in the shipyards at Deptford and Woolwich should be sent up as quickly as possible, along with 'all persons, capable either by hand or judgement to assist in the preservation of the Tower'.

Although there was not as yet much evidence of it, organised action to halt the fire was beginning to get under way. At some point on Monday King Charles decided the crisis called for more forceful interference than that which could be provided by the Earl of Craven and his Coldstream Guards. Not only was the fire spreading more or less unchecked, but public order threatened to break down completely, with gridlock and chaos at the gates, and looting, robberies and savage violence on the streets. (Indeed, up to this point Craven's Guards had spent most of their time rescuing innocent foreigners from lynchings and beatings.) If ever a civil emergency called for military rule, this was it.

As Captain-General of the Kingdom, the Duke of Albemarle, George Monck, was the obvious person to lead the operation. He was also Lord Lieutenant of Middlesex, and thus one of the men responsible for mustering the local militias. But Monck was seventy-five miles away on the Isle of Wight, assessing the damage to his tattered fleet, and it would be several days before he could be recalled. Nor was it clear that he *should* be recalled. When news of the fire reached Holland – and it would, very soon – the Dutch might press home their advantage with an attack on the south coast: bringing home one half of the naval high command (and the sensible half, at that) at such a crucial stage in the war was not a good idea. That very day Monck and Rupert were busy dispatching letters to Charles and James explaining why they had failed to engage with the Dutch on Saturday night. Still unaware of what was happening in London, they blithely asked the Duke of York as Lord High Admiral 'to send what fire ships and other ships you can hither for us, and provisions for us at the Buoy of the Nore, and command the Victualler at Portsmouth to furnish us with everything there'.

With Monck unavailable, Charles II placed his brother in charge. The Duke of York was always happiest in a crisis; Sir William Coventry, who in addition to being a Navy Commissioner was his Secretary at the Admiralty, was quite right when he said that James was 'more himself and more of judgement is at hand in him in the middle of a desperate service, than at other times'. He spent most of Monday riding up and down the crowded streets of the City with his Guards in an attempt to maintain public order, rescuing foreigners from the mob and encouraging localised firefighting efforts. He called in at the Navy Office, where Pepys heard he was 'now General, and having the care of all'. And as Monday wore on with no sign of either the flames or the gales subsiding, he began to prepare a coordinated strategy for containing the fire.

James's plan was simple. He decided to set up command posts with teams of firefighters all round the perimeter of the fire. Aside from the Tower, where John, Lord Berkeley was begging for naval workers to come and help, the most strategic points were in the western suburbs, which were now most likely to bear the brunt of the advancing flames. There were five major posts, beginning with Temple Bar at the west end of Fleet Street and arcing north and east to form a cordon which ran through Clifford's Inn Gardens, Fetter Lane and Shoe Lane, before ending with a station in the little thoroughfare of Cow Lane, which lay between Holborn Conduit and West Smithfield. Each was manned by parish constables, who were ordered to bring with them 100 men apiece. Each of the firefighting teams thus formed was supported – or kept at its post – by a troop of thirty foot soldiers under the command of an officer; and rations of bread, cheese and beer to the value of £5 were provided at each position.* James also installed three courtiers at each station, with orders to reward with a shilling any man who stayed at his post and worked hard throughout the night. Three advance posts were set up closer to the flames, at Aldersgate, Cripplegate and Coleman Street; they were commanded by two gentlemen apiece. The appearance on the front line of so many nobility and gentry was meant to set a good example to the frightened and disorganised citizens; and, no doubt, to provide leadership by men on whom James felt he could rely. But there was another reason for their presence: labourers, constables and aldermen were still reluctant to bring down houses for fear of being held responsible. Perhaps at the Duke's insistence, Charles gave the courtiers manning the fire posts the authority to order demolitions.

Temple Bar had a particular significance. The gatehouse marked not only the junction of Fleet Street and the Strand, but also the point at which

---

* It isn't clear if these provisions were intended just for the night. If they were, it was a generous gesture, since £5 would have allowed each man two loaves, two pounds of ordinary cheese and three gallons of small beer. But then firefighting was thirsty work.

the City's jurisdiction in the western suburbs
ended, and that of Westminster began. It was up
to the men at the Temple Bar fire post to prevent
the fire breaking through and moving up the
Strand to the gates of Whitehall itself. They were
supervised by Lord Belasyse, the absentee Governor
of Tangier and one of the Duke's most trusted
friends; by Hugh May, the Paymaster of the King's
Works, who was currently acting up as Surveyor-
General during Sir John Denham's bout of
madness; and by Thomas Chicheley, a Commissioner of the Ordnance. May was forty-four; the
other two men were both in their early fifties.
The Cow Lane station was commanded by Sir
Richard Browne; Colonel John Fitzgerald, a
Catholic soldier and until 1665 the Deputy-
Governor of Tangier, was in charge of Coleman
Street. Bludworth was at Cripplegate.

James himself tended to move back and forth
between the different posts, but he spent much
of his time in and around Fleet Street. He hoped
that the Fleet River would form a natural firebreak between Ludgate Hill and the affluent
western suburbs leading to Whitehall and Westminster, and decided he and his own men should
make a stand of sorts south of the Fleet Bridge,
in Bridewell and down to the Thames; while the
Earl of Craven would command the firefighting

efforts from Holborn Bridge down to the Fleet Bridge – a defensive line more than half a mile long. Holding that line would be hard, but all hope now rested on it.

The exodus of refugees had continued all through Monday, and by nightfall the ground just beyond the Duke of York's cordon was covered with a pathetic forest of makeshift shelters and dotted with little piles of belongings and furniture. Hatton Garden, an open area to the north-west of the City where over the past few years houses had begun to appear, was filled with people's goods; so were Lincoln's Inn Fields and Gray's Inn Fields, and the tracts of open land around the squalid tenements of St Giles's Fields. The Duke and Lord Arlington told the City to call out two companies of militia to patrol these areas in an attempt to prevent looting.

It took some time to put all of these structures in place. John Evelyn, for example, was sent to help at Fetter Lane; but, if his memory served him well, he didn't actually arrive there until some time on Wednesday. And even on Monday night, when the fire posts were all manned to some extent and everyone was preparing like soldiers in the trenches for the flames to reach them, James was still anxious that he hadn't done enough. From his Whitehall lodgings he told Sir William

Coventry that justices and deputy lieutenants must summon more workmen and tools to arrive on the front line at dawn; and that surrounding churches and chapels must be searched for fire-hooks, 'which should be brought ready upon the place to-night against the morning'.

Then he waited.

5

THE FIRE PROGRESSES

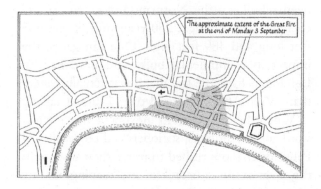

The approximate extent of the Great Fire at the end of Monday 3 September

Once the fire had crossed both Cheapside and the Fleet, it was only a matter of time before St Paul's Cathedral at the top of Ludgate Hill was threatened. St Paul's was the City's most revered landmark. It was London's own cathedral, at whose altar each Lord Mayor prayed for guidance on the day of his installation. But it was more than this – a godly fortress, a divine bulwark against misfortune, of greater significance at an emotional level than the City churches, the Exchange or the Guildhall or any of the Company Halls. Its destruction was unthinkable.

As it happened, there was a precedent for the fate which was about to befall St Paul's. The cathedral, which had been founded more than a thousand years earlier by St Mellitus, first Bishop of London, was destroyed by fire in 1087. It had been rebuilt by the Normans and extended and enlarged over the next 250 years until it was 585 feet long and 489 feet high. One can gauge the impact its monumental bulk must have had on Londoners from the fact that it was actually longer than Wren's cathedral, and over 120 feet taller.

When the fire began its inexorable move westward and the printers, stationers and booksellers of Paternoster Row rushed to move their stock into the crypt of the cathedral for safe keeping, no one thought that St Paul's would come to any serious harm. Even when the surrounding streets began to burn on Tuesday 4 September – Old Change and Lambeth Hill, Foster Lane and Warwick Lane – the monumental stone edifice rose above the smoke, impervious and immortal. William Taswell later recalled that 'the people who lived contiguous to St Paul's church raised their expectations greatly concerning the absolute security of that place upon account of the immense thickness of its walls and its situation; built in a large piece of ground, on every side remote from houses'. They followed the example of the booksellers and filled the cathedral and its surrounding yard with household goods. Every opening into the book-filled crypt was blocked, so that not even the tiniest spark could enter.

Soon after sunset on Tuesday night William Taswell walked across from his school down to Westminster Stairs, over a mile away from St Paul's, where he looked across Lambeth Marsh towards the City. For more than an hour he stood and watched the fire creep around the cathedral, getting closer all the time, until only the firebreak of Paul's Churchyard stood in its way. At eight o'clock he saw flames appear on the roof.

The demolition work had blocked most of the narrow alleys and lanes round about, making it difficult for firefighters to approach with their ladders and buckets. And what if they did? St Paul's was no row of timber-framed houses to be pulled down with hooks; the nave alone stood about 150 feet high. And within less than half an hour the fire spreading along its roof was melting the lead, so that it dripped and then cascaded down into the body of the cathedral, 'as if it had been snow before the sun'. The stonework split and popped and crashed down with explosive force. The lead ran down Ludgate Hill in a stream, 'the very pavements glowing with fiery rednesse, so as no horse nor man was able to tread on them'. As the mountains of tightly packed books and bundles of paper in the crypt caught, the whole building went up with a huge roar, and by nine o'clock the blaze was so bright that it lit up the entire sky. Still standing on Westminster Stairs, William Taswell could see to read an edition of Terence which he had in his pocket. *Hinc illae lacrimae.*★

Londoners had three theories about what had happened. Inevitably, some people thought the cathedral had been fire-bombed. Another school held that the furniture and bedding which had been dragged out of people's houses and piled up against the walls in Paul's Churchyard had caught fire, and that the flames had broken through the windows of the cathedral, igniting the household goods inside and, eventually, the warehoused books and paper in St Faith's. The fire then spread up the scaffolding poles and deal boards to the roof.

A more likely notion was that the wind carried embers from the burning houses below up to the roof of St Paul's. Once the poles and planking on the temporary sections of the south transept roof had caught, the precarious stone vaulting

★ 'Hence these tears' (Terence, *Andria*, l. 26).

close by gave way and fell through the floor into the crypt below, followed by burning scaffold masts and timbers. Exposed to fire and air, the contents of St Faith's went up like a bomb, gutting the interior of the cathedral in less than an hour. The most plausible explanation of all was a two-pronged attack, with both the roof and the goods in Paul's Yard catching fire at much the same time.

Forty miles away in Oxford, the moon turned blood red that night, and there was a distant sound like the waves of the sea. As St Paul's collapsed in ruins, the fashionable shops of Ludgate Hill burned. So did Ludgate itself. The ancient gatehouse, rebuilt in 1586, had a statue of the mythical King Lud facing towards the City and St Paul's, and another of Queen Elizabeth I looking west. It also housed a prison for petty criminals in its upper storey. Deserted by their gaolers, the prisoners broke out, as did the occupants of Newgate Gaol nearby. Elizabeth turned yellow in the heat but remained in one piece, staring out across Lambeth Marsh to Westminster and Whitehall. The poet John Crouch imagined her mixed emotions as her palace was saved while her capital burned:

Though fancy makes not Pictures live, or love,
Yet Pictures fancy'd may the fancy move:

Me-thinks the Queen on White-hall cast
  her Eye;
An Arrow could not more directly flye.
But when she saw her Palace safe, her fears
Vanish, one Eye drops smiles, the other tears.

Even while Elizabeth wept and St Paul's burned and cracked in the heat, the Duke of York was struggling to prevent the western spread of the fire. It had now moved into the Temple, and men were pulling down houses around Somerset House in an effort to form a firebreak on the Strand. If that didn't work, there was nothing to stop the fire reaching the Palace of Whitehall itself; and that night work began on demolishing a set of lodgings built for Sir John Denham in Great Scotland Yard. They lay just by Charing Cross, and looked onto the builders' yards and offices that formed part of the Office of the King's Works. They would also be the first part of the Palace to burn should the fire arrive. Workers were told that the stores of timber stacked in the yards were to be thrown into the Thames. As a precaution, Catherine of Braganza, the Duchess of York and their households began to prepare to leave Whitehall for Hampton Court at dawn the following morning. 'Oh, the confusion there was then at that Court!' wrote Evelyn.

While their servants gathered their clothes and jewellery and packed it into chests, there was another sound above the roar of the flames. The eastern sector of the City shook to an explosion. Then another, and another.

After waiting all day for the workmen from the naval dockyards to arrive, John, Lord Berkeley and his men at the Tower had decided to take matters into their own hands. Military engineers from the Office of Ordnance began to set charges in the houses close by on Tower Street. As they lit train after train of powder, the ground shook, and buildings flew apart or rose a few feet into the air before falling with a strangely muted crump. And there was more panic, as word went round that the cannon in the Tower were firing indiscriminately into the streets. 'Nothing can be like unto the distraction we were in,' wrote one of the Duke's helpers, 'but the Day of Judgement.'

Around eleven o'clock that night, the wind veered to the south. Then it began to die.

6

THE DAMAGE

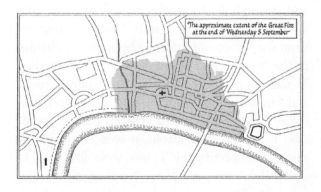

The approximate extent of the Great Fire at the end of Wednesday 5 September

The bare statistics of loss are terrible. A survey carried out soon after the Fire found that 13,200 houses had been burned down or demolished in 400 streets and courts. That meant that somewhere in the region of 70,000–80,000 people had lost their homes. Of the area within the walls, 373 acres had gone – well over 80 per cent – along with a further 63 acres in the extra-mural parishes to the north and west. Eighty-six churches were either badly damaged or completely destroyed. Thirty-five would never be rebuilt, and it would take more than half a century and well over £360,000 to replace the rest – a colossal amount of money in an age when Pepys paid his cook £5 a year, and 5 shillings would buy a roast beef dinner for four in a tavern.

'Of particular men's losses could never be made any computation,' said Clarendon: and he was right. The stationers were generally held to have suffered the most. Many were bankrupted in the destruction of St Paul's Cathedral, when stock worth between £150,000 and £200,000 burned – a catastrophe for the history of English publishing and, in John Evelyn's words, 'an extraordinary detriment to the whole Republiq of Learning'. The consequences for individual businesses are mentioned here and there, but the overall scale of the financial disaster is well-nigh impossible to calculate, although there were plenty who tried. The figure of £600,000 a year in lost rents was mentioned to Pepys in the week after the Fire, but this was certainly an exaggeration and it was soon revised down to around £330,000. Taking the value of each house as twelve years' purchase (i.e., twelve times its annual rent, an estimate which was thought at the time to be fair but conservative), this would suggest that the 13,200 burned houses alone were worth £3.96 million, without even taking account of their contents. And that figure, of course, excludes the value of London's public buildings. In

1681 Thomas Delaune's *Present State of London* reckoned £3.9 million for lost housing, and £2 million apiece for public buildings destroyed, the cost of moving goods about, and the destruction or looting of goods. This gave a grand total of £9.9 million.

A more detailed estimate appeared in John Strype's 1720 edition of Stow's *Survey of the Cities of London and Westminster*. Strype offered a total figure of £10,788,500, but this is too high: the combined rebuilding costs of St Paul's Cathedral and the City churches, for example, are given as £2,696,000, when the figure was around the £1 million mark. The real sum was perhaps somewhere nearer to £9 million, but one can only agree with the Earl of Clarendon when he said that 'the value or estimate of what that devouring fire consumed, over and above the houses, could never be computed in any degree'.

With the loss of the Guildhall, the Exchange and St Paul's, the City's political, commercial and religious centres had disappeared. The destruction of the Custom House and the Excise Office severely impaired its ability to bring in fresh revenues; the burning of the General Letter Office disrupted its lines of communication with the rest of the kingdom; and the loss of most of the Company Halls threatened the social and economic structures which underpinned it.

The support networks which the Livery Companies provided for indigent members were also at risk. Most of the Companies owned rental or lease-hold property, and its destruction led to a diminution of income for various trusts and pensions. The Vintners lost almost all their property; pensioners in Stoke Newington and St George's Fields who were dependent on the Drapers' Company had their pensions reduced from 6s 8d a month to 4s, 'until it shall please God, by some means, to supply the said loss'.

On the other hand, the Companies that survived the Fire relatively unscathed were quick to see an opportunity to turn the situation to their profit, while helping their fellow liverymen at the same time. The Cooks' Company's Tudor Hall on Aldersgate Street was singed, but otherwise unharmed. On 14 September workmen were summoned 'to putt that parte of the Hall and Gallery which is now defaced by the late fire in good repaire', and £11 was paid out for repairing and reglazing the windows, which had presumably cracked and broken in the heat. On the same day the Cooks decided to let their Hall to any other Company which needed a place to meet. The Haberdashers took them up on their offer. So did the Salters, the Bowyers, the Brewers, the Distillers, the Farriers, the Fruiterers, the Glovers, the Painter-Stainers, the Stationers, the Upholders [upholsterers], the Goldsmiths – and the Society for the Propagation of the Gospel.

The Carpenters, who had had the good fortune to escape with their Hall and virtually all of their property intact, were just as quick to offer help to Companies which had suffered 'by the late and dredfull fire'. By the beginning of October the Drapers had stumped up £30 a year for the use of certain rooms on a specified number of days, as had the Masons, the Feltmakers, the Weavers and the Haberdashers, who seem to have tired of the Cooks' Hall rather quickly. The Carpenters also managed to rent out most of their Hall and the surrounding garden to Sir Thomas Bludworth, who, with only a few weeks of his Mayoralty left to run, no longer had the use of Vintners' Hall as his official residence. Three of Bludworth's successors as Lord Mayor continued the arrangement at an annual rent of £100.

With accommodation in short supply, those lucky enough to own houses in the unburned parts of the capital were more than willing to make them available – at a price. On Friday, Pepys had heard of an acquaintance accepting £150 for a house he had previously let at £40 a year. The next day people were starting to comment on the demand for property in the western suburbs. 'Houses are now at an excessive rate,' Edward Atkyns told his brother, Sir Robert; '& my Lord Treasurers new buildings are now in great request.' Atkyns was referring to speculative housing put up in fashionable Bloomsbury Square in the early 1660s by Thomas Wriothesley, 4th Earl of Southampton. Five days later the *Gazette* for 13 September announced that 'The Grand Office for the Excise is now kept in Southampton-Fields, near the House of the Right Honourable the Lord High Treasurer of England, and is every day open at the usual hours, for receiving and performing all things relating to that Affair.'

Edward advised Sir Robert to keep his goods in his house, the implication being that if he didn't, he might find that house occupied by someone else when he next came up to town. And there is evidence to suggest that unscrupulous landlords didn't hesitate to turn the situation to their advantage. While the City still smouldered, Sir Nathaniel Hobart and his wife, Anne, found themselves facing eviction from their substantial house in Chancery Lane, in spite of paying a heavy rental of £55 a year. Luckily for the Hobarts, Sir Nathaniel knew the law (he was a Master in Chancery); and he immediately threatened to slap an injunction on his landlord – 'a person so odious', he said, 'that if his cause were just he would hardly find favour'.★

★ The housing shortage was still causing problems several years later. In August 1668 Pietro Mocenigo, the new Venetian Ambassador, complained to his masters about the 'grasping habits' of Londoners, the 'severe and exorbitant rents' and the difficulty of finding a suitable residence because the Fire 'has left many convenient houses mere heaps of ruins and rubble' (*CSP Venetian*, XXXV, 240, 260). The Doge and Senate took him seriously enough to raise his allowance.

One point made by a number of writers in the days after the Fire was that it could have been worse. Joseph Williamson's 'short, but true accompt' of the disaster in the *Gazette*, which he managed to get out on Monday 10 September, stressed that the warehouses at the east end of Thames Street were filled with goods that were bulky but not particularly valuable. Their loss was regrettable, but 'the other parts of the Town, where the Commodities were of greater value, took the Alarm so early, that they saved most of their Goods'. Given Williamson's role as government spokesperson, we might dismiss this as propaganda. But he was not the only one determined to find a silver lining in the pall of smoke hanging over London. The anonymous author of a private letter to Viscount Conway, who was absent from his townhouse off Drury Lane, was also at pains to say that 'the greatest part of the wealth is saved, the losse having chiefly fallen upon heavy goods, Wine Tobacco Sugars, etc.' However, even Williamson could not resist a swipe at Londoners' selfishness: 'some think, that if the whole industry of the Inhabitants had been applyed to the stopping of the fire, and not to the saving of their particular goods, the success might have been much better, not only to the publick, but to many of them in their own particulars'.

★

As silver linings go, the brightest and best was the size of the casualty list. It was tiny. For Bishop Gilbert Burnet, 'the most astonishing circumstance of that dreadful conflagration was that, notwithstanding the great destruction that was made, and the great confusion in the streets, I could never hear of any one person that was either burnt or trodden to death. The king was never observed to be so much struck with any thing in his whole life, as with this.' Burnet was writing years after the event, and his memory played him false – but not that false. A contemporary pamphleteer was much nearer the mark when he said he could find no evidence for more than half a dozen deaths.

There *were* fatalities, but considering the cataclysmic scale of the disaster and the densely populated areas that were affected, it seems little short of a miracle that they were so few. There was Farriner's maid, who couldn't bring herself to clamber out of an upstairs window; and the 'old decrepid woman' whose charred corpse William Taswell had stumbled over in the ruins of St Paul's. Sixteen months later Pepys was told by a bookseller that several dogs were found burned in Paul's Churchyard 'and but one man', an old man who had gone into the cathedral to retrieve a blanket and had been overcome by the flames. This sounds very much like Taswell's old woman: since her clothes were all burned and her limbs charred, it must have been difficult to determine her sex.

A deaf old Strasbourg watchmaker named Paul Lawell who lived in Shoe Lane refused point-blank to leave his home, in spite of the advice of his son and his friends; he died when his house collapsed on top of him and crashed down into the cellar, 'where afterwards his Bones, together with his Keys, were found'. A parishioner of St Botolph Aldgate dropped dead from fright on Tower Hill. A few others died when floors gave way as they were searching through the ruins of their homes. And that was it. The third-largest city in the Western world burns to the ground and, if contemporaries are to be believed, the death toll is in single figures.

No doubt some deaths went unrecorded, as the poet John Tabor implied in his 'Seasonable Thoughts in Sad Times':

How many frighted Parents now miscarry,
And travail must, at home they may not
    tarry! . . .
How many dying persons now expire!
Breathing their last like Martyrs in the fire . . .
How many dead have Roman buryal there!
Their Houses funeral piles wherein they were

Now burned, and lie buried underneath
The ruins of the place, where seiz'd by death.

Describing the initial outbreak in Pudding Lane, John Dryden wrote of 'frighted mothers [who] strike their breast too late / For helpless infants left amidst the fire'; and one can't help wondering if he was referring to some now-forgotten tragedy. John Evelyn talked vaguely of 'the stench that came from some poore creatures bodies, beds and other combustible goods' as he walked through the ruins on Friday: although he didn't actually *see* a single corpse. And the Fire continued to kill long after the first week in September. The most pathetic death was that of Richard Yrde, who was overcome by fumes while he sat in a privy in the parish of St Mary Woolnoth. The most poignant was that of the seventy-year-old poet and dramatist James Shirley, who was burned out of his home in Fleet Street and forced to shelter in one of the makeshift refugee camps in St Giles-in-the-Fields; he died there eight weeks later and was buried on 29 October. His wife died on the same day, and they were buried in the same grave.

It is hard to believe that there was not a single casualty among the firefighters – especially when firefighting involved pulling down buildings and blowing up buildings. But all the evidence suggests that the death rate really was negligible. The Earl of Clarendon made no mention at all of fatalities in his account of the Fire, and marvelled that no foreigners were killed in spite of the brutal treatment being meted out by the mob: 'It cannot be enough wondered at, that in this general rage of the people no mischief was done to the strangers, that no one of them was assassinated outright, though many were sorely beaten and bruised.' And Thomas Vincent – who positively revelled in describing his face-to-face encounters with dead and dying plague victims – distinguished clearly between those 'who have fallen by the plague' and those 'whose houses have fallen by the fire', implying that 1665 was charac-terised by human losses, while in September 1666 property was the chief casualty.

How could that be?

The first thing to bear in mind is that low mortality rates were not unusual in seventeenth-century urban fires. When flames destroyed well over 200 houses in Warwick on 5 September 1694, the only fatalities were a dozen pigs which were burned in their sties. A fire that burned at least twenty-five houses in Dorchester, Dorset, in January 1622 claimed just a single life, and even there it was helped along by an overzealous citizen. The victim, a tile-layer named Edward

Benebenewe, was badly burned and ran home in a panic, pursued by friends who were trying to calm him down. Mistaking poor Benebenewe for an escaping criminal, a passer-by who just happened to be carrying a pole 'beat him with it grievously and struck him down, he died within two days'.

The Warwick and Dorchester fires both began in the early afternoon, which helps to explain why damage was largely confined to property. The fact that the Fire of London broke out in the early hours should, in theory, have meant casualties; and a contemporary pamphleteer highlighted as one of the main reasons for the magnitude of the disaster 'the Time wherein it did happen, to wit, about One of the Clock in the Night, when every one is buried in his first Sleep; when some for Weariness, others by Deboistness, have given Leave to their Cares to retire; when Slothfulness and the Heat of the Bed have riveted a Man to his Pillow, and made him almost incapable of waking, much less of acting and helping his Neighbours'. But the alarm was raised very quickly; and the Fire spread very slowly. Between the early hours of Sunday and Wednesday morning, it moved westward from Pudding Lane along the Thames at a remarkably consistent rate – around thirty yards per hour. (It tailed off considerably in the course of Wednesday afternoon when, with the exception of flare-ups in the Temple and around Cripplegate, it had to all intents and purposes been extinguished.) Thirty yards per hour is not only the average rate over the three-and-a-half days; it is also true for each full day – Sunday, Monday and Tuesday. The eastward track of the flames against the prevailing wind was of course much slower – no more than six or seven yards per hour – and the spread to the north was less consistent, varying between nine and sixteen yards per hour.

These figures are crude, and they make little allowance for the realities of the situation: the speed with which the flames could travel down one street before dwindling away almost to nothing in the next; the fact that one house might go up like a bomb while another smouldered for days; the way in which fires could break out without warning hundreds of yards apart.

But the fact remains that most people had plenty of time to evacuate their homes. Even on Fish Street, which backed onto Pudding Lane and was one of the first casualties, the occupants were able to save their personal possessions. In the early stages of the Fire, when people still believed that it was a localised outbreak, those close to the perimeter of the fire zone packed up and moved only a few streets away, a process which they repeated again and again. On Sunday morning, for instance, Pepys had run into a merchant, Isaac Houblon, who was standing at the door of his house in Dowgate, supervising the arrival of his brother's goods. They had been moved twice already that day, and Houblon was quite right when he told Pepys that 'they must in a little time be removed from his house also'. Most of Dowgate Hill was burning by nightfall.

Today, the majority of fire-related fatalities are the result of smoke inhalation. This was not necessarily true in the seventeenth century, when the treatment of surface burns relied on little more than the application of honey and prayers. But death and injury from fire had much the same preconditions in 1666 as they do today; and chief among these were the element of surprise and the lack of an escape route. By dawn on Sunday 2 September most of the City knew there was a serious fire; and many were already taking steps to escape. Even though the flames never reached the Strand, on Wednesday morning its occupants 'fled with their families out of their houses in the streets, that they might not be within when the fire fell upon their houses'.

7

EXTRACT FROM THE DIARY
OF JOHN EVELYN

September 2: This fatal night about ten, began that deplorable fire, neere Fish-streete in Lond: 2: I had pub: prayers at home: after dinner the fire continuing, with my Wife & Sonn took Coach & went to the bank side in Southwark, where we beheld that dismal speectaccle, the whole Citty in dreadfull flames neere the Water side, & had now consumed all the houses from the bridge all Thames Streete & up-wards towards Cheape side, downe to the three Cranes, & so returned exceedingly astonishd, what would become of the rest: 3 The Fire having continud all this night (if I may call that night, which was as light as day for 10 miles round about after a dreadfull manner) when consp[ir]ing with a fierce Eastern Wind, in a very drie season, I went on foote to the same place, when I saw the whole South part of the Citty burning from Cheape side to the Thames, & all along Cornehill (for it likewise kindled back against the Wind, as well [as] forward) *Tower-Streete*, *Fen-church*-streete, *Gracious Streete*, & so along to Bainard Castle, and was now taking hold of St. *Paules-Church*, to which the Scaffalds contributed exceedingly: The Conflagration was so universal, & the people so astonish'd, that from the beginning (I know not by what desponding or fate), they hardly stirr'd to quench it, so as there was nothing heard or seene but crying out & lamentation, & running about like distracted creatures, without at all attempting to save even their goods; such a strange consternation there was upon them, so as it burned both in breadth & length, The Churches, Publique Halls, Exchange, Hospitals, Monuments, & ornaments, leaping after a prodigious manner from house to house & streete to streete, at greate distance one from the other, for the heate (with a long set of faire & warme weather) had even ignited the aire, & prepared the materials to conceive the fire, which devoured after a[n] incredible manner, houses, furniture & everything: Here we saw the Thames coverd with goods floating, all the barges & boates laden with what some had time & courage to save, as on the other, the Carts &c carrying out to the fields, which for many miles were strewed with moveables of

all sorts, & Tents erecting to shelter both people
& what goods they could get away: ô the miserable & calamitous speectacle, such as happly
the whole world had not seene the like since
the foundation of it, nor to be out don, 'til the
universal Conflagration of it, all the skie were of
a fiery aspect, like the top of a burning Oven, &
the light seene above 40 miles round about for
many nights: God grant mine eyes may never
behold the like, who now saw above ten thousand
houses all in one flame, the noise & crakling &
thunder of the impetuous flames, the shreeking of
Women & children, the hurry of people, the fall
of towers, houses & churches was like an hideous
storme, & the aire all about so hot & inflam'd that
at the last one was not able to approch it, so as
they were force'd [to] stand still, and let the flames
consume on which they did for neere two whole
mile[s] in length and one in bredth: The Clowds
also of Smoke were dismall, & reached upon
computation neere 50 miles in length: Thus I left
it this afternoone burning, a resemblance of Sodome,
or the last day: It call'd to mind that of 4 *Heb: non
enim hic habemus stabilem Civitatem*: the ruines resem-
bling the picture of *Troy: London* was, but is no
more: Thus I return'd:

4. The burning still rages; I went now on horse
back, & it was now gotten as far as the Inner

Temple; all *Fleetestreete*, old baily, Ludgate hill,
Warwick Lane, Newgate, Paules Chaine, Wattling-
streete now flaming & most of it reduc'd to ashes,
the stones of *Paules* flew like granados, the Lead
mealting downe the streetes in a streame, & the
very pavements of them glowing with fiery
rednesse, so as nor horse nor man was able to
tread on them, & the demolitions had stopped all
the passages, so as no help could be applied; the
Easter[n] Wind still more impetuously driving
the flames forewards: Nothing but the almighty
power of God was able to stop them, for vaine
was the help of man: on the fift it crossed towards
White-hall, but ô the Confusion was then at that
Court: It pleased his *Majestie* to command me
among the rest to looke after the quenching of
fetter-lane end, to preserve (if possible) that part
of *Holborn*, whilst the rest of the Gent: tooke
their several posts, some at one part, some at
another, for now they began to bestirr themselves,
& not 'til now, who 'til now had stood as men
interdict, with their hands a crosse, & began to
consider that nothing was like to put a stop, but
the blowing up of so many houses, as might make
a [wider] gap, than any had yet ben made by the
ordinary method of pulling them downe with
Engines; This some stout Seamen proposd early
enought to have saved the whole Citty; but some

tenacious & avaritious Men, Aldermen &c. would
not permitt, because their houses must have ben
[of] the first: It was therefore now commanded
to be practised, & my concerne being particularly
for the *Hospital* of st. *Bartholomeus* neere Smithfield,
where I had many wounded & sick men, made
me the more diligent to promote it; nor was my
care for the *Savoy* lesse: So as it pleased Almighty
God by abating of the Wind, & the industrie of
people, now when all was lost, infusing a new
Spirit into them (& such as had if exerted in time
undoubtedly preserved the whole) that the furie
of it began sensibly to abate, about noone, so as
it came no farther than the Temple West-ward,
nor than the enterance of Smithfield North; but
continued all this day & night so impetuous toward
Cripple-Gate, & The Tower, as made us even all
despaire; It also brake out againe in
the Temple: but the courage of the multitude
persisting, & innumerable houses blown up with
Gunpowder, such gaps & desolations were soone
made, as also by the former three days consump-
tion, as the back fire did not so vehemently urge
upon the rest, as formerly: There was yet no
standing neere the burning & glowing ruines neere
a furlongs Space; The Coale & Wood wharfes &
magazines of Oyle, rozine, [chandler] &c: did
infinite mischiefe; so as the invective I but a little

The Diary of John Evelyn

before dedicated to his Majestie & publish'd,* giving warning what might probably be the issue of suffering those shops to be in the Citty, was lookd on as prophetic: but there I left this smoking & sulltry heape, which mounted up in dismall clowds night & day, the poore Inhabitans dispersd all about St. Georges, Moore filds, as far as higate, & severall miles in Circle, Some under tents, others under miserab[l]e Hutts and Hovells, without a rag, or any necessary utinsils, bed or board, who from delicatnesse, riches & easy accommodations in stately & well furnishd houses, were now reduc'd to extreamest misery & poverty: In this Calamitous Condition I returnd with a sad heart to my house, blessing & adoring the distinguishing mercy of God, to me & mine, who in the midst of all this ruine, was like *Lot*, in my little Zoar, safe and sound:

6 Thursday, I represented to his Majestie the Case, of the French Prisoners at War in my Custodie, & besought him, there might be still the same care of Watching at all places contiguous to unseized houses: It is not indeede imaginable how extraordinary the vigilanc[e] & activity of the King & Duke was, even labouring in person, & being present, to command, order, reward, and

* *Fumifugium.*

75

encourage Workemen; by which he shewed his affection to his people, & gained theirs: Having then disposed of some under Cure, at the Savoy, I return'd to white hall, where I dined at Mr. *Offleys*, Groome-porter, who was my relation, together with the *Knight Martial*, where I also lay that night.

7 I went this morning on foote from White hall as far as *London* bridge, thro the Late fleete streete, Ludgate hill, by St. Paules, Cheape side, Exchange, Bishopsgate, Aldersgate, & out to Morefields, thence thro Cornehill, &c: with extraordinary difficulty, clambring over mountaines of yet smoking rubbish, & frequently mistaking where I was, the ground under my feete so hott, as made me not onely Sweate, but even burnt the soles of my shoes, & put me all over in Sweate. In the meane time his Majestie got to the *Tower* by Water, to demolish the houses about the Graft, which being built intirely about it, had they taken fire, & attaq'd the white Towre, where the Magazines of Powder lay, would undo[u]btedly have not onely beaten downe & destroyed all the bridge, but sunke & torne all the vessels in the river, & rendred the demolition beyond all expression for severall miles even about the Country at many miles distance: At my returne I was infinitly concern'd to find that goodly Chur[c]h St. *Paules*

now a sad ruine, & that beautifull Portico (for structure comparable to any in Europ, as not long before repaird by the late King) now rent in pieces, flakes of vast Stone Split in sunder, & nothing remaining intire but the Inscription in the *Architrave* which shewing by whom it was built, had not one letter of it defac'd: which I could not but take notice of: It was astonishing to see what imense stones the heate had in a manner Calcin'd, so as all the ornaments, Columns, freezes, Capitels & proje[c]tures of massie Portland stone flew off, even to the very roofe, where a Sheete of Leade covering no lesse than 6 akers by measure, being totaly mealted, the ruines of the Vaulted roofe, falling brake into St. Faithes, which being filled with the magazines of bookes, belonging to the Stationer[s], & carried thither for safty, they were all consumed burning for a weeke following: It is also observable, that the lead over the Altar at the East end was untouch'd; and among the divers monuments, the body of one *Bishop*, remaind intire. Thus lay in ashes that most venerab[l]e Church, one of the [antientest] Pieces of early Piety in the Christian World, beside neere 100 more; The lead, yronworke, bells, plate &c mealted; the exquisitely wrought Mercers Chapell, the Sumptuous Exchange, the august fabricque of Christ church, all the rest of the

Companies Halls, sumptuous buildings, Arches, Enteries, all in dust. The fountaines dried up & ruind, whilst the very waters remained boiling; the Voragos of subterranean Cellars Wells & Dungeons, formerly Ware-houses, still burning in stench & dark clowds of smoke like hell, so as in five or six miles traversing about, I did not see one loade of timber unconsum'd, nor many stones but what were calcind white as snow, so as the people who now walked about the ruines, appeard like men in some dismal desart, or rather in some greate Citty, lay'd wast by an impetuous & cruel Enemy, to which was added the stench that came from some poore Creaturs bodys, beds, & other combustible goods: Sir *Tho: Gresshams* Statue, though falln to the ground from its nich in the Ro: Exchange remain'd intire, when all those of the Kings since the Conquest were broken to pieces: also the Standard in Cornehill, & *Q: Elizabeths* Effigies, with some armes on Ludgate continud with but little detriment, whilst the vast yron Chaines of the Cittie streetes, vast hinges, barrs & gates of Prisons were many of them mealted, & reduc'd to cinders by the vehement heats: nor was I yet able to passe through any of the narrower streetes, but kept the widest, the ground & aire, smoake & fiery vapour, continud so intense, my haire being almost seinged, & my feete unsufferably surbated: The bielanes & narrower streetes were quite fill'd up with rubbish, nor could one have possibly knowne where he was, but by the ruines of some church, or hall, that had some remarkable towre or pinacle remaining: I then went towards Islington, & highgate, where one might have seene two hundred thousand people of all ranks & degrees, dispersed, & laying along by their heapes of what they could save from the *Incendium*, deploring their losse, & though ready to perish for hunger & destitution, yet not asking one penny for reliefe, which to me appeard a stranger sight, than any I had yet beheld: His *Majestie* & Council indeeade tooke all imaginable care for their reliefe, by Proclamation, for the Country to come in & refresh them with provisions: when in the middst of all this Calamity & confusion, there was (I know not how) an *Alarme* begun, that the *French* & *Dutch* (with whom we were now in hostility) were not onely landed, but even entring the Citty; there being in truth, greate suspicion some days before, of those two nations joyning, & even now, that they had ben the occasion of firing the Towne: This report did so terrifie, that on a suddaine there was such an uprore & tumult, that they ran from their goods, & taking what weapons they could come at, they could not be stop'd from

falling on some of those nations whom they
casualy met, without sense or reason, the clamor
& perill growing so excessive, as made the whole
Court amaz'd at it, & they did with infinite paines,
& greate difficulty reduce & appease the people,
sending Guards & troopes of souldiers, to cause
them to retire into the fields againe, where they
were watched all this night when I left them
pretty quiet, & came home to my house, suffi-
ciently weary and broken: Their spirits thus a little
sedated, & the affright abated, they now began
to repaire into the suburbs about the Citty, where
such as had friends or opportunit[i]e got shelter
& harbour for the Present; to which his Majesties
Proclamation also invited them. Still the Plage,
continuing in our parish, I could not without
danger adventure to our Church. 10: I went againe
to the ruines, for it was now no longer a Citty:
11 Sat at Star Chamber, on the 13, I presented
his Majestie with a Survey of the ruines, and a
Plot for a new Citty, with a discourse on it,
whereupon, after dinner his Majestie sent for me
into the Queenes Bed-chamber, her Majestie &
the Duke onely present, where they examind each
particular, & discoursd upon them for neere a full
houre, seeming to be extreamly pleasd with what
I had so early thought on: The *Queene* was now
in her *Cavaliers* riding habite, hat & feather &

horsemans Coate, going to take the aire; so I tooke leave of his Majestie & visiting the *Duke* of *Albemarle*, now newly return'd from Sea, I went home. 15 To *Lond:* & dined with my L: *Brounchar* president of our Society, where was also the Earle of *Clancarne*, Sir *Rob: Murray,* & Dr. *Christopher Wrenn.* 16 *Pomeridiano* I went to Greenewich church, when Mr. *Plume* preached very well on *Pet: Seing therefore all these things must be disolvd* &c: 19: To *Star-Chamber,* returnd at night; 23: To *Greenewich*, where the Minister proceeded on his former Text: 25 To *Lond:* to Star: cha: 26. Din'd at Sir W: *Boremans.* 27: at Sir William *D'Oylies* with that worthy Gent: Sir *Jo: Holland* of Suffolck, & Mr. *Scaven*, sat with our Commissioners for sick & Wounded, & returned home. 29 *Michaelmas-day,* I went to visite my *Bro: Richard*, who was now indisposd in his health:

October 2: I gave my Bro: of *Wotton* a Visite, being myselfe also not well, & returnd the 4th, so as I entred into a Course of Steele, against the *Scorbut*:

10 This day was indicted a Generall fast through the nation, to humble us, upon the late dreadfull Conflagration, added to the Plage & Warr, the most dismall judgments could be inflicted, & indeede but what we highly deserved for our prodigious ingratitude, burning Lusts, disolute

Court, profane & abominable lives, under such dispensations of Gods continued favour, in restoring Church, Prince, & people from our late intestine calamities, of which we were altogether unmindfull even to astonishment: This made me resolve to go to our Parish Assemblie, where our Doctor preached on 19 Luke: 41 &c: piously applying it to the occasion, after which followd a Collection for the poore distressd loose[r]s in the late fire, & their present reliefe. 14: He preached on 9: *Dan:* 14:

18 To *Lond:* Star-Chamber: thence to Court, it being the first time of his *Majesties* putting himselfe solemnly into the *Eastern fashion* of Vest, changing doublet, stiff Collar, [bands] & Cloake &c: into a comely Vest, after the *Persian* mode with girdle or shash, & Shoe strings & Garters, into bouckles, of which some were set with precious stones, resolving never to alter it, & to leave the French mode, which had hitherto obtained to our greate expense & reproch: upon which divers Courtiers & Gent: gave his Ma[jesty] gold, by way of Wager, that he would not persist in this resolution: I had some time before indeede presented an Invectique against that unconstancy, & our so much affecting the french fashion, to his Majestie in which [I] tooke occasion to describe the Comelinesse & usefullnesse of the Persian clothing in the very same manner, his Majestie

clad himselfe; This Pamphlet I intituled *Tyrannus* or the mode, & gave it his Majestie to reade; I do not impute the change which soone happn'd to this discourse, but it was an identitie, that I could not but take notice of: This night was acted my Lord *Brahals* Tragedy cal'd *Mustapha* before their Majesties &c: at Court: at which I was present, very seldom at any time, going to the publique *Theaters,* for many reasons, now as they were abused, to an atheisticall liberty, fowle & undecent; Women now (& never 'til now) permitted to appeare & act, which inflaming severall young noble-men & gallants, became their whores, & to some their Wives, wittnesse the *Earle* of *Oxford,* Sir R: Howard, Pr: Rupert, the E: of Dorset, & another greater person than any of these, who fell into their snares, to the reproch of their noble families, & ruine both of body & Soule: I was invited to see this Tragedie, exceedingly well writ, by my Lord Chamberlain, though in my mind, I did not approve of any such passe time, in a season of such Judgements & Calamitie: 19 I return'd home;

21 Our *Viccar* on his former subject: This season (after so long & extraordinary a drowth in September, & Aug: as if preparatory for the dreadfull fire) was so very wett & rainy, as many feared an ensuing famine.

8

EXTRACT FROM THE DIARY
OF SAMUEL PEPYS

September 1666

2. *Lords day*. Some of our maids sitting up late last night to get things ready against our feast today, Jane called us up, about 3 in the morning, to tell us of a great fire they saw in the City. So I rose, and slipped on my nightgown and went to her window, and thought it to be on the back side of Markelane at the furthest; but being unused to such fires as fallowed, I thought it far enough off, and so went to bed again and to sleep. About 7 rose again to dress myself, and there looked out at the window and saw the fire not so much as it was, and further off. So to my closet to set things to rights after yesterday's cleaning. By and by Jane comes and tells me that she hears that above 300 houses have been burned down tonight by the fire we saw, and that it was now burning

down all Fishstreet by London Bridge. So I made myself ready presently, and walked to the Tower and there got up upon one of the high places, Sir J. Robinsons little son going up with me; and there I did see the houses at that end of the bridge all on fire, and an infinite great fire on this and the other side the end of the bridge – which, among other people, did trouble me for poor little Michell and our Sarah on the Bridge. So down, with my heart full of trouble, to the Lieutenant of the Tower, who tells me that it begun this morning in the King's bakers house in Pudding lane, and that it hath burned down St Magnes Church and most part of Fishstreete already. So I down to the waterside and there got a boat and through the bridge, and there saw a lamentable fire. Poor Michells house, as far as the Old Swan, already burned that way and the fire running further, that in a very little time it got as far as the Stillyard while I was there. Everybody endeavouring to remove their goods, and flinging into the River or bringing them into lighters that lay off. Poor people staying in their houses as long as till the very fire touched them, and then running into boats or clambering from one pair of stair by the waterside to another. And among other things, the poor pigeons I perceive were loath to leave their houses, but hovered about the windows and balconies till they were some of them burned, their wings, and fell down.

Having stayed, and in an hour's time seen the fire rage every way, and nobody to my sight endeavouring to quench it, but to remove their goods and leave all to the fire; and having seen it get as far as the Steeleyard, and the wind mighty high and driving it into the city, and everything, after so long a drougth, proving combustible, even the very stones of churches, and among other things, the poor steeple by which pretty Mrs [Horsley] lives, and whereof my old schoolfellow Elborough is parson, taken fire in the very top and there burned till it fall down – I to Whitehall with a gentleman with me who desired to go off from the Tower to see the fire in my boat – to Whitehall, and there up to the King's closet in the chapel, where people came about me and I did give them an account dismayed them all; and word was carried in to the King, so I was called for and did tell the King and Duke of York what I saw, and that unless his Majesty did command houses to be pulled down, nothing could stop the fire. They seemed much troubled, and the King commanded me to go to my Lord Mayor from him and command him to spare no houses but to pull down before the fire every way. The Duke of York bid me tell him that if he would have any more soldiers, he shall; and so did my Lord Arlington afterward, as a great secret. Here meeting with Capt. Cocke, I in his coach, which he lent me, and Creed with me, to Pauls; and there walked along Watling street as well as I could, every creature coming away loaden with goods to save – and here and there sick people carried away in beds. Extraordinary good goods carried in carts and on backs. At last met my Lord Mayor in Canning Streete, like a man spent, with a handkercher about his neck. To the King's message, he cried like a fainting woman, 'Lord, what can I do? I am spent! People will not obey me. I have been pull[ing] down houses. But the fire overtakes us faster then we can do it.' That he needed no more soldiers; and that for himself, he must go and refresh himself, having been up all night. So he left me, and I him, and walked home – seeing people all almost distracted and no manner of means used to quench the fire. The houses too, so very thick thereabouts, and full of matter for burning, as pitch and tar, in Thames street – and warehouses of oyle and wines and Brandy and other things. Here I saw Mr Isaccke Houblon, that handsome man – prettily dressed and dirty at his door at Dowgate, receiving some of his brothers things whose houses were on fire; and as he says, have been removed twice already, and he doubts (as it soon proved) that they must be in a little time removed from his house also – which was a sad consideration. And to see the churches all filling with goods, by people who themselfs should have been quietly there at this time. By this time it was about 12 a-clock, and so home and there find my guests, which was Mr Wood and his wife, Barbary Shelden, and also Mr Moone – she mighty fine, and her husband, for aught I see, a likely man. But Mr Moones design and mine, which was to look over my closet and please him with the sight thereof, which he hath long desired, was wholly disappointed, for we were in great trouble and disturbance at this fire, not knowing what to think of it. However, we had an extraordinary good dinner, and as merry as at this time we could be. While at dinner, Mrs Batelier came to enquire after Mr Woolfe and Stanes (who it seems are related to them), whose houses in Fishstreet are all burned, and they in a sad condition. She would not stay in the fright.

As soon as dined, I and Moone away and walked through the City, the streets full of nothing but people and horses and carts loaden with goods, ready to run over one another, and removing goods from one burned house to another – they now removing out of Canning street (which received goods in the morning) into Lumbard Streete and further; and among others, I now saw my little goldsmith Stokes receiving some friend's goods, whose house itself was burned the day after. We parted at Pauls, he home and I to Pauls Wharf, where I had appointed a boat to attend me; and took in Mr Carcasse and his brother, whom I met in the street, and carried them below and above bridge, to and again, to see the fire, which was now got further, both below and above, and no likelihood of stopping it. Met with the King and Duke of York in their Barge, and with them to Queen Hith and there called Sir Rd. Browne to them. Their order was only to pull down houses apace, and so below bridge at the waterside; but little was or could be done, the fire coming upon them so fast. Good hopes there was of stopping it at the Three Cranes above, and at Buttolphs Wharf below bridge, if care be used; but the wind carries it into the City, so as we know not by the waterside what it doth there. River full of lighter[s] and boats taking in goods, and good goods swimming in the water; and only, I observed that hardly one lighter or boat in three that had goods of a house in, but there was a pair of virginalls in it. Having seen as much as I could now, I away to Whitehall by appointment, and there walked to St James's Park, and there met my wife and Creed and Wood and his wife and walked to my boat, and there upon the water again, and to the fire up and down, it still increasing and the wind great. So near the fire as we could for smoke; and all over the Thames, with one's face in the wind you were almost burned with a shower of Firedrops – this is very true – so as houses were burned by these drops and flakes of fire, three or four, nay five or six houses, one from another. When we could endure no more upon the water, we to a little alehouse on the Bankside over against the Three Cranes, and there stayed till it was dark almost and saw the fire grow; and as it grow darker, appeared more and more, and in Corners and upon steeples and between churches and houses, as far as we could see up the hill of the City, in a most horrid malicious bloody flame, not like the fine flame of an ordinary fire. Barbary and her husband away before us. We stayed till, it being darkish, we saw the fire as only one entire arch of fire from this to the other side of the bridge, and in a bow up the hill, for an arch of above a mile long. It made me weep to see it. The churches, houses, and all on fire and flaming at once, and a horrid noise the flames made, and the cracking of houses at their ruine.

So home with a sad heart, and there find

everybody discoursing and lamenting the fire; and poor Tom Hater came with some few of his goods saved out of his house, which is burned upon Fish street hill. I invited him to lie at my house, and did receive his goods: but was deceived in his lying there, the noise coming every moment of the growth of the Fire, so as we were forced to begin to pack up our own goods and prepare for their removal. And did by Mooneshine (it being brave, dry, and moonshine and warm weather) carry much of my goods into the garden, and Mr Hater and I did remove my money and Iron chests into my cellar – as thinking that the safest place. And got my bags of gold into my office ready to carry away, and my chief papers of accounts also there, and my tallies into a box by themselfs. So great was our fear, as Sir W. Batten had carts come out of the country to fetch away his goods this night. We did put Mr Hater, poor man, to bed a little; but he got but very little rest, so much noise being in my house, taking down of goods.

3. About 4 a-clock in the morning, my Lady Batten sent me a cart to carry away all my money and plate and best things to Sir W. Riders at Bednall greene; which I did, riding myself in my nightgown in the Cart; and Lord, to see how the

streets and the highways are crowded with people, running and riding and getting of carts at any rate to fetch away thing[s]. I find Sir W. Rider tired with being called up all night and receiving things from several friends. His house full of goods – and much of Sir W. Batten and Sir W. Penn's. I am eased at my heart to have my treasure so well secured. Then home with much ado to find a way. Nor any sleep all this night to me nor my poor wife. But then, and all this day, she and I and all my people labouring to get away the rest of our things, and did get Mr Tooker to get me a lighter to take them in, and we did carry them (myself some) over Tower hill, which was by this time full of people's goods, bringing their goods thither. And down to the lighter, which lay at the next quay above the Tower dock. And there was my neighbour's wife, Mrs [Buckworth], with her pretty child and some few of her things, which I did willingly give way to be saved with mine. But there was no passing with anything through the postern, the crowd was so great. The Duke of York came this day by the office and spoke to us, and did ride with his guard up and down the City to keep all quiet (he being now General, and having the care of all). This day, Mercer being not at home, but against her mistress order gone to her mother's, and my wife going thither to speak with W. Hewer, met her there and was angry; and her mother saying that she was not a prentice girl, to ask leave every time she goes abroad, my wife with good reason was angry, and when she came home, bid her be gone again. And so she went away, which troubled me; but yet less then it would, because of the condition we are in fear of coming into in a little time, of being less able to keep one in her quality. At night, lay down a little upon a quilt of W. Hewer in the office (all my own things being packed up or gone); and after me, my poor wife did the like – we having fed upon the remains of yesterday's dinner, having no fire nor dishes, nor any opportunity of dressing anything.

4. Up by break of day to get away the remainder of my things, which I did by a lighter at the Iron gate; and my hands so few, that it was the afternoon before we could get them all away. Sir W. Penn and I to Tower street, and there met the fire Burning three or four doors beyond Mr Howells; whose goods, poor man (his trayes and dishes, Shovells &c., were flung all along Tower street in the kennels, and people working therewith from one end to the other), the fire coming on in that narrow street, on both sides, with infinite fury. Sir W. Batten, not knowing how to remove

his wind, did dig a pit in the garden and laid it in there; and I took the opportunity of laying all the papers of my office that I could not otherwise dispose of. And in the evening Sir W. Penn and I did dig another and put our wine in it, and I my parmazan cheese as well as my wine and some other things. The Duke of York was at the office this day at Sir W. Penn's, but I happened not to be within. This afternoon, sitting melancholy with Sir W. Penn in our garden and thinking of the certain burning of this office without extraordinary means, I did propose for the sending up of all our workmen from Woolwich and Deptford yards (none whereof yet appeared), and to write to Sir W. Coventry to have the Duke of York's permission to pull down houses rather then lose this office, which would much hinder the King's business. So Sir W. Penn he went down this night, in order to the sending them up tomorrow morning; and I wrote to Sir W. Coventry about the business, but received no answer.

This night Mrs Turner (who, poor woman, was removing her goods all this day – good goods, into the garden, and knew not how to dispose of them) – and her husband supped with my wife and I at night in the office, upon a shoulder of mutton from the cook's, without any napkin or anything, in a sad manner but were merry. Only, now and then walking into the garden and saw how horridly the sky looks, all on a fire in the night, was enough to put us out of our wits; and endeed it was extremely dreadfull – for it looks just as if it was at us, and the whole heaven on fire. I after supper walked in the dark down to Tower street, and there saw it all on fire at the Trinity house on that side and the Dolphin tavern on this side, which was very near us – and the fire with extraordinary vehemence. Now begins the practice of blowing up of houses in Tower street, those next the Tower, which at first did frighten people more then anything; but it stop[ped] the fire where it was done – it bringing down the houses to the ground in the same places they stood, and then it was easy to quench what little fire was in it, though it kindled nothing almost. W. Hewer this day went to see how his mother did, and comes late home, but telling us how he hath been forced to remove her to Islington, her house in Pye Corner being burned. So that it is got so far that way and all the Old Bayly, and was running down to Fleet street. And Pauls is burned, and all Cheapside. I wrote to my father this night; but the post-house being burned, the letter could not go.

5. I lay down in the office again upon W. Hewer's quilt, being mighty weary and sore in my feet

with going till I was hardly able to stand. About 2 in the morning my wife calls me up and tells of new Cryes of 'Fyre!' – it being come to Barkeing Church, which is the bottom of our lane. I up; and finding it so, resolved presently to take her away; and did, and took my gold (which was about 23 50*l*), W. Hewer, and Jane down by Poundy's boat to Woolwich. But Lord, what a sad sight it was by moonlight to see the whole City almost on fire – that you might see it plain at Woolwich, as if you were by it. There when I came, I find the gates shut, but no guard kept at all; which troubled me, because of discourses now begun that there is plot in it and that the French had done it. I got the gates open, and to Mr Shelden's, where I locked up my gold and charged my wife and W. Hewer never to leave the room without one of them in it night nor day. So back again, by the way seeing my goods well in the lighters at Deptford and watched well by people. Home, and whereas I expected to have seen our house on fire, it being now about 7 a-clock, it was not. But to the Fyre, and there find greater hopes then I expected; for my confidence of finding our office on fire was such, that I durst not ask anybody how it was with us, till I came and saw it not burned. But going to the fire, I find, by the blowing up of houses and the great help given by the workmen out of the King's yards, sent up by Sir W. Penn, there is a good stop given to it, as well at Marke lane end as ours – it having only burned the Dyall of Barkeing Church, and part of the porch, and was there quenched. I up to the top of Barkeing steeple, and there saw the saddest sight of desolation that I ever saw. Everywhere great fires. Oyle cellars and brimstone and other things burning. I became afeared to stay there long; and therefore down again as fast as I could, the fire being spread as far as I could see it, and to Sir W. Penn's and there eat a piece of cold meat, having eaten nothing since Sunday but the remains of Sunday's dinner.

Here I met with Mr Young and Whistler; and having removed all my things, and received good hopes that the fire at our end is stopped, they and I walked into the town and find Fanchurch street, Gracious street, and Lumbard street all in dust. The Exchange a sad sight, nothing standing there of all the statues or pillars but Sir Tho. Gresham's picture in the corner. Walked into Moorefields (our feet ready to burn, walking through the town among the hot coles) and find that full of people, and poor wretches carrying their goods there, and everybody keeping his goods together by themselfs (and a great blessing it is to them that it is fair weather for them to keep abroad night and day); drank there, and paid twopence for a plain penny loaf. Thence homeward, having passed through Cheapside and Newgate market, all burned – and seen Anthony Joyces house in fire. And took up (which I keep by me) a piece of glass of Mercer's chapel in the street, where much more was, so melted and buckled with the heat of the fire, like parchment. I also did see a poor Catt taken out of a hole in the chimney joyning to the wall of the Exchange, with the hair all burned off the body and yet alive. So home at night, and find there good hopes of saving our office – but great endeavours of watching all night and having men ready; and so we lodged them in the office, and had drink and bread and cheese for them. And I lay down and slept a good night about midnight – though when I rose, I hear that there had been a great alarme of French and Duch being risen – which proved nothing. But it is a strange thing to see how long this time did look since Sunday, having been alway full of variety of actions, and little sleep, that it looked like a week or more. And I had forgot almost the day of the week.

6. Up about 5 a-clock, and there met Mr Gawden at the gate of the office (I entending to go out, as I used every now and then to do, to see how

the fire is) to call our men to Bishoppsgate, where no fire had yet been near, and there is now one broke out – which did give great grounds to people, and to me too, to think that there is some kind of plott in this (on which many by this time have been taken, and it hath been dangerous for any stranger to walk in the streets); but I went with the men and we did put it out in a little time, so that that was well again. It was pretty to see how hard the women did work in the cannells sweeping of water; but then they would scold for drink and be as drunk as devils. I saw good Butts of sugar broke open in the street, and people go and take handfuls out and put into beer and drink it. And now all being pretty well, I took boat and over to Southwarke, and took boat on the other side the bridge and so to Westminster, thinking to Shift myself, being all in dirt from top to bottom. But could not there find any place to buy a Shirt or pair of gloves, Westminster hall being full of people's goods – those in Westminster having removed all their goods, and the Exchequer money put into vessels to carry to Nonsuch. But to the Swan, and there was trimmed. And then to Whitehall, but saw nobody, and so home. A sad sight to see how the River looks – no houses nor church near it to the Temple – where it stopped. At home did go with

Sir W. Batten and our neighbour Knightly (who, with one more, was the only man of any fashion left in all the neighbourhood hereabouts, they all removing their goods and leaving their houses to the mercy of the fire) to Sir R. Ford's, and there dined, in an earthen platter a fried breast of mutton, a great many of us. But very merry; and endeed as good a meal, though as ugly a one, as ever I had in my life. Thence down to Deptford, and there with great satisfaction landed all my goods at Sir G. Carteret's, safe, and nothing missed I could see, or hurt. This being done to my great content, I home; and to Sir W. Batten's and there with Sir R. Ford, Mr Knightly, and one Withers, a professed lying rogue, supped well; and mighty merry and our fears over. From them to the office and there slept, with the office full of labourers, who talked and slept and walked all night long there. But strange it was to see Cloathworkers hall on fire these three days and nights in one body of Flame – it being the cellar, full of Oyle.

7. Up by 5 a-clock and, blessed be God, find all well, and by water to Paul's wharfe. Walked thence and saw all the town burned, and a miserable sight of Pauls church, with all the roofs fallen and the body of the Quire fallen into St Fayths – Paul's school also – Ludgate – Fleet street – my

father's house, and the church, and a good part of the Temple the like. So to Creeds lodging near the New Exchange, and there find him laid down upon a bed – the house all unfurnished, there being fears of the fire's coming to them. There borrowed a shirt of him – and washed. To Sir W. Coventry at St James's, who lay without Curtains, having removed all his goods – as the King at Whitehall and everybody had done and was doing. He hopes we shall have no public distractions upon this fire, which is what everybody fears – because of the talk of the French having a hand in it. And it is a proper time for discontents – but all men's minds are full of care to protect themselfs and save their goods. The Militia is in armes everywhere. Our fleetes, he tells me, have been in sight of one another, and most unhappily by Fowle weather were parted, to our great loss, as in reason they do conclude – the Duch being come out only to make a show and please their people; but in very bad condition as to stores, victuals, and men. They are at Bullen, and our fleet come to St Ellens. We have got nothing, but have lost one ship, but he knows not what.

Thence to the Swan and there drank; and so home and find all well. My Lord Brouncker at Sir W. Batten's, and tells us the Generall is sent for up to come to advise with the King about business at this juncture, and to keep all quiet – which is great honour to him, but I am sure is but a piece of dissimulation. So home and did give order for my house to be made clean; and then down to Woolwich and there find all well. Dined, and Mrs Markeham came to see my wife. So I up again, and calling at Deptford for some things of W. Hewer, he being with me; and then home and spent the evening with Sir R. Ford, Mr Knightly, and Sir W. Penn at Sir W. Batten's. This day our Merchants first met at Gresham College, which by proclamation is to be their Exchange. Strange to hear what is bid for houses all up and down here – a friend of Sir W. Riders having 150*l* for what he used to let for 40*l* per annum. Much dispute where the Custome house shall be; thereby the growth of the City again to be foreseen. My Lord Treasurer, they say, and others, would have it at the other end of the town. I home late to Sir W. Penn, who did give me a bed – but without curtains or hangings, all being down. So here I went the first time into a naked bed, only my drawers on – and did sleep pretty well; but still, both sleeping and waking, had a fear of fire in my heart, that I took little rest. People do all the world over cry out of the simplicity of my Lord Mayor in general, and more perticularly in this business of the fire, laying it all upon him. A proclamation is come out for markets to be kept at Leadenhall and Mile end greene and several other places about the town, and Tower hill, and all churches to be set open to receive poor people.

8. Up, and with Sir W. Batten and Sir W. Penn by water to Whitehall, and they to St James's. I stopped with Sir G. Carteret, to desire him to go with us and to enquire after money. But the first he cannot do, and the other as little, or says, 'When can we get any, or what shall we do for it?' He, it seems, is imployed in the correspondence between the City and the King every day, in settling of things. I find him full of trouble to think how things will go. I left him, and to St James's, where we met first at Sir W. Coventry's chamber and there did what business we can without any books. Our discourse, as everything else, was confused. The fleet is at Portsmouth, there staying a wind to carry them to the Downes or toward Bullen, where they say the Duch fleete is gone and stays. We concluded upon private meetings for a while, not having any money to satisfy any people that may come to us. I bought two eeles upon the Thames, cost me 6s. Thence with Sir W. Batten to the Cockpit, whither the

Duke of Albemarle is come. It seems the King holds him so necessary at this time, that he hath sent for him and will keep him here. Endeed, his interest in the City, being acquainted, and his care in keeping things quiet, is reckoned that wherein he will be very serviceable. We to him. He is courted in appearance by everybody. He very kind to us. I perceive he lays by all business of the fleet at present and minds the City, and is now hastening to Gresham College to discourse with the Aldermen. Sir W. Batten and I home (where met by my Brother John, come to town to see how things are with us). And then presently he with me to Gresham College – where infinite of people; partly through novelty to see the new place, and partly to find out and hear what is become one man of another. I met with many people undone, and more that have extraordinary great losses. People speaking their thoughts variously about the beginning of the fire and the rebuilding of the City. Then to Sir W. Batten and took my brother with me, and there dined with a great company of neighbours, and much good discourse; among others, of the low spirits of some rich men in the City, in sparing any encouragement to the poor people that wrought for the saving their houses. Among others, Ald. Starling, a very rich man, without children, the fire at next door to him in our Lane – after our men had saved his house, did give 2*s*. 6*d*. among 30 of them, and did quarrel with some that would remove the rubbish out of the way of the fire, saying that they came to steal. Sir. W. Coventry told me of another this morning in Holborne, which he showed the King – that when it was offered to stop the fire near his house for such a reward, that came but to 2*s*. 6*d*. a man among the neighbours, he would give but 18*d*. Thence to Bednall green by coach, my brother with me, and saw all well there and fetched away my Journall-book to enter for five days past. To the office, and late writing letters; and then to Sir W. Penn, my brother lying with me, and Sir W. Penn gone down to rest himself at Woolwich. But I was much frighted, and kept awake in my bed, by some noise I heard a great while below-stairs and the boys not coming up to me when I knocked. It was by their discovery of people stealing of some neighbours' wine that lay in vessels in the street. So to sleep. And all well all night.

9. *Sunday*. Up, and was trimmed, and sent my brother to Woolwich to my wife to dine with her. I to church, where our parson made a melancholy but good sermon – and many, and most, in the church cried, especially the women. The

church mighty full, but few of fashion, and most strangers. I walked to Bednall green; and there dined well, but a bad venison pasty, at Sir W. Rider's. Good people they are, and good discourse. And his daughter Middleton, a fine woman and discreet. Thence home, and to church again, and there preached Deane Harding; but methinks a bad poor sermon, though proper for the time – nor eloquent, in saying at this time that the City is reduced from a large Folio to a Decimo tertio. So to my office, there to write down my journall and take leave of my brother, whom I sent back this afternoon, though rainy – which it hath not done a good while before. But I had no room nor convenience for him here till my house is fitted; but I was very kind to him, and do take very well of him his journey. I did give him 40*s.* for his pocket; and so he being gone, and it presently rayning, I was troubled for him, though it is good for the Fyre. Anon to Sir W. Penn to bed, and made my boy Tom to read me asleep.

13. Up, and down to Tower wharfe; and there with Balty and labourers from Deptford did get my goods housed well at home. So down to Deptford again to fetch the rest, and there eat a bit of dinner at the Globe, with the maister of the *Bezan* with me, while the labourers went to

dinner. Here I hear that this poor town doth bury still of the plague seven or eight in a day. So to Sir G. Carteret's to work; and there did, to my great content, ship off into the *Bezan* all the rest of my goods, saving my pictures and fine things, that I will bring home in wherrys when my house is fit to receive them. And so home and unloaden them by carts and hands before night, to my exceeding satisfaction; and so after supper to bed in my house, the first time I have lain there; and lay with my wife in my old closet upon the ground, and Balty and his wife in the best chamber, upon the ground also.

14. Up, and to work, having Carpenters come to help in setting up bedsteads and hangings; and at that trade my people and I all the morning, till pressed by public business to leave them, against my will, in the afternoon; and yet I was troubled in being at home, to see all my goods lie up and down the house in a bad condition, and strange workmen going to and fro might take what they would almost. All the afternoon busy; and Sir W. Coventry came to me, and found me, as God would have it, in my office, and people about me setting my papers to rights; and there discoursed about getting an account ready against the Parliament, and thereby did create me infinite of

business, and to be done on a sudden, which troubled me; but however, he being gone, I about it late to good purpose; and so home, having this day also got my wine out of the ground again and set it in my cellar; but with great pain to keep the port[er]s that carried it in from observing the money-chests there. So to bed as last night; only, my wife and I upon a bedstead with curtains in that which was Mercer's chamber, and Balty and his wife (who are here and do us good service) where we lay last night.

15. All morning at the office, Harman being come, to my great satisfaction, to put up my beds and hangings; so I am at rest, and fallowed my business all day. Dined with Sir W. Batten. Mighty busy about this account, and while my people were busy, myself wrote near 30 letters and orders with my own hand. At it till 11 at night; and it is strange to see how clear my head was, being eased of all the matter of all those letters; whereas one would think that I should have been dozed – I never did observe so much of myself in my life. In the evening there comes to me Capt. Cocke, and walked a good while in the garden; he says he hath computed that the rents of houses lost this fire in the City comes to 600000*l* per annum. That this will make the Parliament more quiet

then otherwise they would have been and give the
King a more ready supply. That the supply must
be by excise, as it is in holland. That the Parliament
will see it necessary to carry on the war. That the
late storm hindered our beating the Duch fleet,
who were gone out only to satisfy the people,
having no business to do but to avoid us. That
the French, as late in the year as it is, are coming.
That the Duch are really in bad condition, but
that this unhappiness of ours doth give them
heart. That, certainly, never so great a loss as this
was borne so well by citizens in the world as this;
he believing that not one merchant upon the
Change will break upon it. That he doth not
apprehend there will be any disturbances in estate
upon it, for that all men are busy in looking after
their own business, to save themselfs. He gone, I
to finish my letters; and home to bed and find,
to my infinite joy, many rooms clean, and myself
and wife lie in our own chamber again. But much
terrified in the nights nowadays with dreams of
fire and falling down of houses.

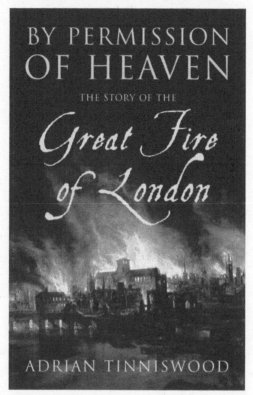

BY PERMISSION
OF HEAVEN

THE STORY OF THE

Great Fire
of London

ADRIAN TINNISWOOD

'Even Pepys is too near and involved an observer to
convey the full magnitude of the catastrophe. For that we
need an historian, and Adrian Tinniswood's new account
of the Great Fire rises impressively to the challenge'
Sunday Telegraph

'Admirably researched and highly evocative'
Spectator

'Vivid, masterly'
Mail on Sunday

penguin.co.uk/vintage